Mithai

Mithai

Indian Sweets Made Easy

KUMUD DWIVEDI

ROLI

CONTENTS

PREFACE

My earliest memories of mithai are inseparable from the texture of life itself – the warmth of family gathered close, the rhythm of festivals returning like old friends and the certainty that something sweet would always be at the centre of it all. A plate of besan ladoos rolled by hand, their fragrance filling the kitchen before they had even cooled. Boxes of barfi and peda exchanged at the door on Diwali, their weight a kind of language all its own.

Mithai, to me, has never been simply dessert. In India, the pleasures of mithai are a great deal more than a pleasant ending to a meal. It is occasion and offering, comfort and celebration, hospitality made edible.

From birth to death, and for everything in between mithai is essential: we use them as sacred offerings to honour and appease gods, mark life's passages, festivals and celebrations. We carry them to visit friends and family, celebrate exam results and they are even part of the lived-in superstitions in India – eating dahi-cheeni (yoghurt and sugar) before taking an exam or appearing for an interview. So much is the sway of sugar on us, that we greet all good news with the ritual of 'Muh meetha karna' (sweetening the mouth). Offering mithai is more than a gesture of hospitality; it is a way of celebrating life's important moments with warmth and affection.

Thousands of sweet shops are crammed across every city, where one can often spot cauldrons of milk being boiled, sweetened, curdled; or watch as the halwai sits frying jalebis in hot oil and dunking them in syrup. The eve of any festival means serpentine queues, everyone waiting for their fix. And every festival carries its own recipes and rituals – some sweets are made once a year, prepared over hours with a ceremonial devotion, others assembled quickly for an unexpected guest, a Tuesday afternoon, a moment that simply called for something sweet. Even now, certain flavours can collapse time entirely: cardamom dissolving into warm milk, the deep nuttiness of ghee in a hot pan, saffron bleeding gold into cream, the gentle percussion of sugar syrup finding its thread.

Ghevar, a popular dessert from Rajasthan, is a common sight in mithai shops with the onset of monsoon.

Over time, my relationship with mithai deepened beyond memory. I found myself absorbed by the craft beneath the sweetness – the alchemy by which a handful of simple ingredients become something luminous. Mithai demands patience and attention, but it is also profoundly intuitive. Much of its knowledge lives not in recipes but in the hands: learned through observation, repetition and a sensitivity to heat and texture that no measurement can fully capture.

Every region of India has its own sweet traditions, shaped by its climate and culture. Bengali sweets are built on the delicate softness of chenna and fresh milk. South Indian sweets sing with coconut, jaggery and rice. In the North, khoya lends its richness to some of the most beloved confections in the country, while the West turns to gram flour, nuts and ghee for its distinctive character. Taken together, these recipes are not merely food – they are a portrait of India's extraordinary culinary imagination.

Yet, tradition and evolution have never been opposites. I believe mithai can be both faithfully preserved and thoughtfully adapted. Modern kitchens are different from the ones in which many of these recipes were born. Throughout this book, I have tried to hold both things at once: to honour the flavours and philosophy of traditional mithai, while offering the substitutions and techniques that make these recipes genuinely achievable.

The recipes gathered here range from sweets that come together in under an hour to more elaborate preparations reserved for festivals and celebrations. Some are faithfully traditional; others have been gently adapted, while others have been re-imagined with healthy, mindful twists.

Whatever your experience with Indian sweets – whether you are encountering mithai for the first time or have spent a lifetime making it – I hope you find something here that speaks to you.

Above all, I hope this book serves as a reminder of what mithai has always been for: sharing. These sweets exist in the context of togetherness – festivals and weddings, religious occasions and ordinary days, the simple human act of handing something sweet to someone you love. To make mithai is to join a tradition that runs deeper than any single recipe, older than any written instruction, carried forward through generations in the most ordinary and extraordinary moments of life.

For families, making mithai at home is often one of the many steps in the long list of preparations for a festival.

Ghee

ON A SWEET NOTE

Techniques, Ingredients and Craft

Indian mithai is a discipline defined by precision, patience and a deep sensitivity to texture and temperature. Rooted in centuries of culinary tradition, yet adaptable across modern kitchens, these confections rely on a set of foundational techniques that, once mastered, allow for both consistency and creativity. I would like to introduce the essential principles that underpin mithai-making, offering a framework for cooks working in diverse environments around the world.

At the heart of many Indian sweets lies sugar syrup, or chashni, whose consistency determines the final texture and structure of the dish. The progression from a light thread consistency to a thicker, more viscous stage requires careful attention, as even slight variations can significantly affect the outcome. In professional kitchens, thermometers provide accuracy, particularly in unfamiliar climates, though traditional methods rely on tactile cues, such as the formation of threads between the fingers. A small amount of acid, often in the form of lemon juice, is commonly introduced to prevent crystallization and ensure a smooth syrup. Maintaining the syrup at a warm, stable temperature – rather than allowing it to boil – is equally critical when soaking fried sweets.

Milk and its transformations form another cornerstone of mithai. Through slow reduction, full-fat milk yields khoya (or mawa), a dense, concentrated base that varies in texture depending on its intended use, from firm and grate-able to soft and smooth. This process demands continuous stirring over controlled heat to prevent scorching and to develop a deep, caramelized flavour. Similarly, preparations such as rabri and kheer rely on gradual evaporation, during which layers of cream are repeatedly folded back into the liquid to build richness. In contrast, fresh cheese such as chenna is created by curdling

Jalebi is one of India's most popular street-side sweets. Golden jalebis taking shape in hot oil, moments before they are immersed in syrup, capture the craft and rhythm of everyday mithai-making.

milk with acid, then gently kneading the solids into a smooth, pliable dough. The degree of kneading directly influences the final texture, particularly in delicate sweets where softness and lightness are prized.

Control of heat is central to every stage of mithai preparation. Frying, for instance, is not a rapid process but a slow and deliberate one, conducted over moderate temperatures to ensure that sweets cook evenly from the inside out. Excessive heat can result in an over-browned exterior and an undercooked interior, compromising both texture and flavour. Roasting, or bhuno, is equally nuanced, requiring patience to coax out the nutty aromas of flours such as gram flour or semolina without tipping into bitterness. As mixtures cook and thicken, visual and tactile cues – such as the mass pulling away cleanly from the sides of the pan – signal readiness. At this point, swift handling is essential, as many sweets must be shaped or cut while still warm to achieve clean, precise finishes.

The quality and understanding of ingredients play a decisive role in the final product. Ghee, with its distinctive aroma and richness, is fundamental to the character of many sweets, while sugar contributes not only sweetness but also structure and shelf stability. Full-fat dairy is preferred for its depth of flavour, though milk powder and other concentrated forms offer practical alternatives in global kitchens. Flours such as gram flour and semolina introduce body and texture, while nuts lend both richness and contrast. Aromatics including cardamom, saffron, rose water and kewra define the signature flavour profile of mithai, used with restraint to create balance rather than excess.

Texture in mithai is guided as much by observation as by measurement. Doughs must achieve a delicate balance – soft enough to shape, yet firm enough to hold structure – while the absorption of syrup depends on both temperature and porosity. Experienced cooks rely on sensory indicators, from the fragrance of roasting ingredients to the subtle shift in consistency as mixtures thicken and set. These cues, developed through repetition, are essential to mastering the craft.

Balancing flavour is particularly important in presenting mithai to a global audience. While richness and sweetness are intrinsic to the tradition, small adjustments – such as the addition of a pinch of salt or a hint of acidity – can enhance complexity and

Mithai is a staple part of religious practices in India. Across the subcontinent, mithai is central to rituals and a common offering to idols or to worshippers as prasad.

Coca-Cola

prevent heaviness. Modern interpretations often moderate sugar levels or use sugar alternatives without compromising structural integrity, resulting in desserts that feel both authentic and refined.

Presentation serves as the final expression of technique. Clean, geometric cuts, restrained garnishing and careful attention to serving temperature elevate mithai from the everyday to the exceptional. Whether served warm, chilled, or at room temperature, each sweet reveals its optimal texture and flavour under specific conditions, underscoring the importance of timing and care.

For cooks working outside the Indian subcontinent, adaptation is both necessary and encouraged. Substitutions such as well-drained ricotta in place of chenna, or evaporated milk in place of reduced milk, can yield credible results when handled thoughtfully. However, adjustments in cooking time, sugar concentration and technique may be required to account for differences in climate, altitude and ingredient composition.

Ultimately, the mastery of mithai lies not in rigid adherence to recipes but in the cultivation of intuition. Techniques must be practiced, observed and refined, allowing the cook to respond instinctively to the subtle changes that occur throughout the process. In this way, the traditions of mithai continue to evolve while remaining grounded in their fundamental principles, offering a confectionery language that is both timeless and universal.

A mithai shop is a familiar sight when strolling through the streets of India. They turn particularly crowded during festivals, as it is tradition to visit loved ones and offer sweets in celebration.

RASGULLA

Syrup-soaked cheese balls

DODHA BARFI

Caramelized milk fudge with nuts

KALAKAND

Milk cake

RASMALAI

Soft discs in saffron milk

RASMALAI TIRAMISU

Rasmalai meets creamy tiramisu

ROSE COCONUT MODAK

Rose-flavoured sweet dumplings

PANCHAMRIT

Blend of milk curd, ghee & honey

PEDA

Rich fudge-like sweet discs

SHEER KHURMA

Vermicelli pudding

SAFFRON SEVIYAN

Vermicelli cooked with saffron

CHENNA PODA

Caramelized milk curd cheesecake

MILK-BASED SWEETS

RASGULLA

SOFT, SYRUP-SOAKED CHEESE BALLS

*

An iconic Bengali sweet celebrated across India, these light paneer balls are gently simmered in sugar syrup until they double in size, absorbing sweetness while retaining a delicate texture.

PREP TIME **20** mins   COOKING TIME **20–25** mins   MAKES **12–15** pcs

INGREDIENTS

500 ml full-fat milk

5 g tartaric acid crystals

1.2 g baking powder

8 g cornflour

250 ml water

500 g sugar

5 ml pandanus (kewra) water

METHOD

1. Heat the milk in a pan over medium heat until it comes to a boil. Cool for a few minutes.
2. Dissolve the tartaric acid in half cup water, and add to the milk gradually, stirring gently until the milk curdles and whey separates. Leave for 2 minutes, then strain through a muslin cloth and wash under cold water to remove the sourness. Squeeze out excess water to get soft paneer.
3. Place the paneer on a clean surface and rub with the palm of your hand to get a soft creamy consistency. Add the baking powder and cornflour and knead for 8–10 minutes until smooth and soft. Divide into 12–15 small portions and make round balls ensuring there are no cracks.
4. For the sugar syrup, bring the sugar and water to a boil in a pot, over medium heat. Keep syrup at a rolling boil. Gently drop the prepared balls into the boiling syrup.
5. Cover and cook on medium flame for 5 minutes. Remove the lid, add a few tablespoons of water, and stir only the top. Repeat this process for about 15–20 minutes. To check when done, take a rasgulla with some syrup in a ladle, if it settles at the bottom, it is done. By this time, the balls will double in size.
6. Add the kewra water once cooked. Remove from heat and leave for one hour. Strain and serve chilled.

DODHA BARFI

CARAMELIZED MILK FUDGE WITH NUTS

*

This North Indian sweet is known for its deep caramelized flavour and slow-cooked richness. The addition of coconut, cocoa malt and ghee lends depth, while nuts add a lovely crunch.

PREP TIME **30** mins | COOKING TIME **1** hr **30** mins | MAKES **20–25** pcs

INGREDIENTS

2 L full-fat milk

300 g sugar

125 g broken wheat (preferably sprouted)

125 g yoghurt

50 ml liquid glucose

100 g dry coconut, grated

100 ml ghee (divided)

20 g Bournvita or any cocoa malt powder

2 g green cardamom powder

50 g almonds, chopped

50 g cashew nuts, chopped

50 g pistachios, chopped

METHOD

1. In large wok, bring the milk to a boil on high heat. Turn down the heat to medium, add the sugar and stir until it is completely dissolved.
2. In a bowl, combine the broken wheat and yoghurt. Gradually add to the milk, while stirring continuously. This will split the milk slightly and give the dodha its grainy texture
3. Cook it for approximately 1 hour on medium heat. Keep scraping the sides and mixing frequently to avoid sticking.
4. Add the liquid glucose, dry coconut, Bournvita and 50 ml ghee. Reduce the heat to low heat and cook for 15–20 minutes, stirring once or twice in between.
5. When it starts to get thick, stir continuously. Add the cardamom powder and continue stirring for 10–15 minutes.
6. When the mix is very thick, add the remaining ghee, chopped almonds and cashew nuts. Mix till it leaves the sides of the pan. Take off the heat.
7. Grease a tray with ghee. Pour the hot mixture, spread evenly and level the surface.
8. Garnish with pistachios, pressing them lightly in to the dodha.
9. Let it cool at room temperature for 6–8 hours. Cut into squares or diamonds and serve.

KALAKAND

MOIST, GRAINY MILK CAKE

Made by reducing full-fat milk and gently curdling it to achieve its signature grainy texture, kalakand strikes a beautiful balance between richness and lightness.

PREP TIME **20** mins (plus resting time)

COOKING TIME **1** hr **30** mins

MAKES **10–12** pcs

INGREDIENTS

2 g alum powder
30 ml water
2½ L full-fat milk
175 gm sugar
2 g green cardamom powder
20 ml ghee
Pistachios, chopped for garnish

METHOD

1. In a small bowl, dissolve the alum in 30 ml water. Keep aside.
2. Heat the milk in a wok over high heat. Bring the milk to a boil, stirring continuously. Turn the heat down to medium and stir and reduce till the milk is about 1.5 L.
3. Now, reduce the heat to low and sprinkle a little alum water on the milk, while stirring. Cook for a few minutes, then sprinkle a little alum water again. Keep cleaning the sides of the wok with another spoon. Repeat this process till the milk becomes granular in texture.
4. Add the sugar and cardamom powder. Continue cooking till reduced further, stirring continuously. The milk is done when it is thick, there is no water on top, and starts leaving the sides of the wok. This will take around 30 minutes.
5. Add the ghee and mix well. Take off the heat.
6. Pour into a greased 8 x 8 inch square mould, level and garnish with pistachios on top.
7. Cover and wrap with a cloth and leave to cool at room temperature for about 8 hours. Cut into small squares or rectangles, and serve.

RASMALAI

SOFT DISCS IN SWEET SAFFRON MILK

*

Soft, spongy paneer balls soaked in saffron- and cardamom-infused rabri in this classic Bengali dessert.

PREP TIME **45** mins
(plus soaking time)

COOKING TIME **40–45** mins

MAKES **10–12** pcs

INGREDIENTS

For the Rasgullas

2 soapnuts (reetha)

5 g citric acid crystals

725 ml water (divided)

1 L cow milk

5 g cornflour

250 g sugar

For the Rabri (Flavoured Milk)

1 L full-cream milk

80 g sugar

5–6 saffron strands

½ tsp green cardamom powder

10 ml rose water

10 g chopped pistachios

10 g almonds

METHOD

1. In a small bowl, soak the reetha in 125 ml water for 2 hours.
2. In another bowl, dissolve the citric acid in 100 ml water. Set aside.
3. Boil the milk in a heavy-bottom pan on high heat. When it starts boiling, reduce the heat to low and slowly add the citric acid solution while stirring gently until the milk curdles.
4. Strain through a muslin cloth and rinse with cold water to remove acidity. Knot the cloth and hang the paneer for 30 minutes to remove excess water.
5. In a mixing bowl, add the paneer and cornflour. Knead lightly until smooth and soft. Divide into 20–25 g portions. Using your hands shape them into balls and flatten slightly.
6. To make the sugar syrup, bring 500 ml water with sugar to a boil in a pot on medium heat. Keep the syrup at a rolling boil.
7. Gently add the paneer balls in the sugar syrup, and add 2 tsp of the reetha water. Cook for 10–15 minutes on medium heat. If the syrup becomes thick, add a little water. To check if done, put a ball in the ladle with the syrup, it should settle at the bottom. Turn off the heat, remove the balls from the syrup and let them cool.
8. For the rabri, boil the milk in a heavy-bottom pan on medium heat. Reduce the milk to about half, stirring occasionally to prevent sticking. This will take about 20–25 minutes.
9. Add the sugar, rose water, saffron and cardamom powder. Mix well. Remove from heat and let it cool slightly. Serve chilled.

RASMALAI TIRAMISU

RASMALAI MEETS CREAMY TIRAMISU

*

This is a delicate fusion of Indian and Italian desserts, combining the cardamom- and saffron-infused rasmalai with the creamy richness of mascarpone and whipped cream.

PREP TIME **25–30** mins CHILLING TIME **4–6** hrs SERVES **6–8**

INGREDIENTS

300 ml whipping cream

250 g mascarpone cheese

100 ml condensed milk

2 g green cardamom powder

Saffron, a few strands, soaked in 1 tbsp warm milk

250 ml rasmalai milk (page 24)

150 g ladyfinger biscuits (savoiardi)

12 pieces rasmalai (page 24), cut into halves

50 g pistachio powder

Rose petals, to garnish

METHOD

1. In a chilled bowl, whip the cream until soft peaks form. Set aside.
2. In another bowl, add the mascarpone, condensed milk, cardamom powder and the saffron-infused milk. Whisk until smooth.
3. Gently fold the whipped cream into the mascarpone mixture. Keep chilled.
4. Place the rasmalai milk in a shallow dish. Briefly dip ladyfingers in the flavoured milk (do not over-soak) and place them in a layer in a serving dish.
5. Spread half the mascarpone cream mixture. Arrange the rasmalai pieces over it. Add the remaining cream mixture.
6. Cover and refrigerate overnight, or for a minimum of 4–6 hours for the flavours to meld. Garnish with pistachio powder. Sprinkle rose petals on top.

ROSE COCONUT MODAK

ROSE-FLAVOURED DUMPLINGS WITH COCONUT

*

Traditionally made during Ganesh Chaturthi, these delicate, fragrant and visually stunning rose coconut modaks are a festive treat that celebrates both flavour and artistry.

PREP TIME **25–30** mins | COOKING TIME **10** mins | MAKES **12–15** pcs

INGREDIENTS

360 ml milk
100 g sugar
235 g desiccated coconut (divided)
30 ml cream
10 g fennel seeds
40 g chopped dry fruits
20 g rose petal preserve (gulkand)
20 g candied cherries, chopped
Rose essence, a few drops
2 g green cardamom powder
1 drop edible red colour
Edible golden dust, for garnish
Fresh rose petals, for garnish

METHOD

1. In a heavy-bottom pan, bring the milk to a gentle boil over medium heat.
2. Add the sugar and stir until fully dissolved. Stir in 200 g desiccated coconut and mix well.
3. Add the cream, and cook on low flame for 1 minute, stirring continuously, until the mixture thickens and leaves the sides of the pan. Turn off the heat and transfer the mixture onto a plate.
4. For the filling, combine 20 g desiccated coconut, fennel seeds, chopped dry fruits, gulkand, chopped candied cherries and a few drops of rose essence in a bowl. Shape into 12–15 small marble-sized balls (about 8–10 g each) and set aside.
5. Divide the milk-coconut mix into two equal parts. Add the cardamom powder to one part and the red colour to the other part.
6. In the modak mould, first fill a small portion of the pink coconut mix, then insert the gulkand ball and cover with the white coconut mix. Press tightly. Demould and place on a tray and repeat with the remaining dough and stuffing.
7. Once shaped, lightly roll the modaks in the reserved 15 g desiccated coconut for a delicate coating, if desired. Dust with edible golden dust and garnish with fresh rose petals. Serve.

PANCHAMRIT

SACRED BLEND OF MILK, CURD, GHEE, HONEY & SUGAR

Offered as prasad in temples and homes, the traditional panchamrit recipe is enriched here with tulsi, nuts, fox nuts, coconut and fragrant rose petals for added texture and aroma.

PREP TIME **10** mins   SERVES **3–4**

INGREDIENTS

180 ml cow milk
120 g cow milk yoghurt
5 ml cow ghee
7 g organic honey
20 g sugar
4–5 holy basil (tulsi) leaves
5 ml Ganga jal or water
10 g almonds, slivered
15 g fox nuts (makhana), roasted
5 g Cuddapah almond (chironji)
5 g raisins
10 g fresh coconut, thinly sliced
2 g dried rose petals

METHOD

1. In a clean bowl (preferably silver or bronze), add the milk, yoghurt, ghee, honey and sugar.
2. Whisk until well blended and the sugar dissolves completely.
3. Add the holy basil leaves, water, almonds, fox nuts, cuddapah almond, raisins, coconut slices and dried rose petals. It is now ready to be served as prasad.

PEDA

RICH, FUDGE-LIKE SWEET DISCS

Soft, milky and gently scented with cardamom, these homemade pedas capture the essence of traditional Indian mithai in its simplest form.

PREP TIME **15** mins | COOKING TIME **30** mins | MAKES **20** pcs

INGREDIENTS

1 tsp cornflour
1 L full-fat milk
80 g sugar
½ tsp cardamom powder
5 ml ghee
30 g pistachios, slivered

METHOD

1. In a small bowl, dissolve the cornflour in 2–3 tbsp cold milk. Keep aside.
2. Pour the milk into a heavy-bottom pan. Bring to a boil on medium heat, stirring occasionally to prevent sticking.
3. Once the milk comes to a boil, reduce the heat to low. Add the dissolved cornflour gradually, stirring continuously. This will help thicken the milk slightly.
4. Add the sugar and stir until dissolved. Add the cardamom powder. Keep stirring and simmer for 25–30 minutes on low heat until the mixture reduces to a thick, fudge-like consistency.
5. Now, add the ghee for shine and richness. Take off the heat.
6. Allow the mixture to cool in the pan for 8–10 minutes, until it is warm but no longer too hot to handle. Transfer it to a zip-lock bag, or a lightly greased tray, and refrigerate for 20–25 minutes, or until firm enough to shape.
7. Once the mixture is cool, remove the mix from the bag. Knead with the heel of the palm until smooth.
8. Grease your palms lightly with ghee, divide the mix into 20 portions, and shape into round pedas.
9. Make an indent in the centre or use the pedal marker to make a design on top. Lightly press the pistachios into the indent and allow the pedas to cool completely. They will firm up as they cool.

SHEER KHURMA

RICH VERMICELLI PUDDING

*

Traditionally prepared for Eid, this dessert is a timeless expression of warmth and celebration.

PREP TIME **25** mins COOKING TIME **25–30** mins SERVES **4–6**

INGREDIENTS

40 g yellow dried dates (chuara)
15 g almonds
10 g pistachios
15 g cashew nuts
45 ml ghee (divided)
40 g golden raisins
100 g long roasted vermicelli (seviyan)
2 green cardamom pods
1 L full-cream milk
75 g sugar (divided)
5 ml rose water
Dried rose petals, for garnish
Silver leaf, for garnish
Chopped nuts, for garnish

METHOD

1. Soak the dates in hot water for 30 minutes, then chop. Slice the almonds, pistachios and cashew nuts into thin slivers.
2. Heat 30 ml ghee in a heavy-bottom pan over medium heat. Fry the cashew nuts, almonds, pistachios for 2–3 minutes, or until golden. Remove and drain on kitchen towels. Set aside.
3. In the same ghee, fry the raisins until they puff up. This will take 1–2 minutes. Remove and keep aside.
4. In another pan over medium heat, add the remaining 15 ml ghee. Add the vermicelli into the pan and lightly crush the into small pieces. Add in the cardamom pods and roast for 3–4 minutes, until golden and fragrant. Remove from heat and set aside.
5. In a large saucepan on high heat, bring the milk to a gentle boil. Then reduce the heat, and simmer for 8–10 minutes, stirring occasionally.
6. Meanwhile, in a small pan, melt 50 g sugar on low heat for 3–4 minutes, or until golden brown. Immediately pour the caramel into the boiling milk and stir quickly. This gives sheer khurma its signature colour and taste.
7. Now, add the roasted vermicelli to the caramelized milk. Simmer for 6–8 minutes until soft. Stir in the remaining 25 g sugar. Add the chopped dates, fried nuts and raisins. Take off the heat and transfer to serving bowls.
8. Garnish with dried rose petals, silver leaf and extra nuts. Serve warm or chilled.

SAFFRON SEVIYAN

VERMICELLI COOKED WITH SAFFRON

Delicately golden and richly aromatic, saffron seviyan is a classic dessert that transforms the humble vermicelli into something quietly luxurious.

PREP TIME **10** mins

COOKING TIME **15** mins

SERVES **4–5**

INGREDIENTS

Saffron, a few strands

30 ml ghee (divided)

150 g long roasted vermicelli (seviyan)

125 ml water

75 g sugar

3 green cardamom pods, lightly crushed

15 g almonds, sliced

15 g cashew nuts, chopped

15 g golden raisins

5 ml rose water

10 g pistachios

METHOD

1. In a small bowl, soak the saffron in 1 tbsp warm water. Allow it to steep while you cook the seviyan.
2. Heat 15 ml ghee in a broad pan on low heat. Once the ghee is hot, add the vermicelli and roast for 3–4 minutes, or until golden and aromatic. Remove and set aside.
3. In the same pan, add water, sugar and cardamom pods and cook on high heat. Stir until the sugar dissolves. Add the saffron water.
4. Turn the heat to low and add the roasted vermicelli into the saffron syrup. Combine well and cook for 4–5 minutes until the liquid is absorbed and the seviyan softens. Remove from heat, cover the pan and leave for 5 minutes.
5. In another small pan on medium flame, heat the remaining ghee. Fry the almonds, cashews and raisins for 2–3 minutes or until golden.
6. Stir the fried nuts and raisins into the seviyan. Add the rose water, garnish with the pistachios and a few saffron strands. Serve warm.

CHENNA PODA

CARAMELIZED MILK CURD CHEESECAKE

Often called the 'burnt cheesecake of Odisha,' chenna poda is a beloved baked dessert that celebrates the magic of slow caramelization. It is traditionally lined with sal leaves for an earthy aroma.

PREP TIME **1** hr **10** mins | COOKING TIME **40–50** mins | SERVES **6–8**

INGREDIENTS

Citric acid, a few crystals
100 ml water
1.5 L full-cream milk
30 g semolina, fine
150 g powdered sugar
1 pinch salt
3 g green cardamom powder
25 ml ghee
2 pinches baking soda
25 g almonds, flaked
25 g pistachios, chopped
Sal leaves, for lining the tin (optional)

METHOD

1. In a small bowl, dissolve the citric acid in 100 ml water.
2. Bring the milk to a boil in a pot over high heat. Take off the heat and let it cool for 2 minutes. Slowly add the citric acid solution, stirring continuously, till the milk curdles and the whey is separated. You may not have to use all of the citric acid solution.
3. Strain the curdled milk through a muslin cloth, and rinse with water. Knot the cloth and hang for 30 minutes to remove excess water. Keep the whey aside. The milk solids so obtained is chenna.
4. Take the soft chenna in a flat bowl and mash it with your palm until smooth.
5. Add the semolina, sugar, salt, cardamom powder, ghee, baking soda and 2–3 tablespoons of reserved chenna water. Mix well into a smooth batter. The texture should be thick but spreadable. Fold in the almonds and pistachios.
6. Grease a 6-inch round baking tin with ghee, or if using sal leaves, arrange them at the bottom, covering the sides of the tin. Pour the mixture and level the top.
7. Bake at 180°C in a preheated oven for 40–50 minutes, or until the top turns golden brown and a skewer inserted comes out clean.
8. Let it cool slightly, then demould. Cut into slices and serve warm or at room temperature.

BESAN BARFI
Gram flour fudge with ghee

BESAN LADOO
Sweet, roasted gram flour ghee balls

GUJIA
Khoya- & nut-filled pastry

MOONG DAL HALWA
Lentil dessert with ghee & nuts

PUNJABI PINNI
Wheat flour balls with ghee & jaggery

CHURMA LADOO
Crumbled wheat flour balls

PARIPPU PAYASAM
Lentil & coconut milk pudding

SEMOLINA LADOO
Semolina balls with ghee & nuts

SOFT MYSORE PAK
Soft, ghee-rich gram flour squares

MOTICHOOR LADOO PARFAIT
Boondi with Greek yoghurt & cream

PURAN POLI
Lentil-stuffed sweet flatbreads

FLOUR & LENTIL-BASED SWEETS

BESAN BARFI

GRAM FLOUR FUDGE WITH GHEE

A classic Indian sweet made by patiently roasting gram flour in ghee until it turns golden and nutty – this barfi develops deep, caramelized flavours that form the heart of the recipe.

PREP TIME **15** mins | COOKING TIME **35–40** mins | MAKES **20–24** pcs

INGREDIENTS

200 ml ghee
400 g gram flour (besan)
300 g sugar
160 ml water
Saffron, a few strands
2 g green cardamom powder
30 g pistachios, slivered

METHOD

1. Heat a heavy-bottom wok on low flame. Add the ghee, and let it melt completely.
2. Add the besan gradually, stirring constantly to avoid any lumps. Roast on low heat for 25–30 minutes until the mixture turns golden, aromatic, and starts releasing ghee. Keep stirring continuously to prevent burning.
3. In a saucepan over medium heat, combine the sugar with water. Cook until the sugar dissolves completely.
4. Add the saffron and cardamom, and continue boiling until the syrup reaches one-string consistency (the syrup forms a single, thin, unbroken thread when pressed between your thumb and forefinger when it is cooled slightly), or when checked with a thermometer, the temperature is 105°C. This will take 3–5 minutes.
5. Add the prepared sugar syrup into the roasted besan slowly while stirring. Remove from heat and mix thoroughly so the syrup combines evenly with the roasted besan.
6. Immediately transfer the mixture into a greased tray. Level it with a spatula. Sprinkle the pistachios on top and press lightly so they stick.
7. Allow the mixture to cool at room temperature for 3–4 hours. Once set, cut into square or diamond-shaped pieces.

BESAN LADOO

ROASTED GRAM FLOUR BALLS

Warm, fragrant and irresistibly rich, besan ladoo is a timeless North Indian sweet. Often prepared for festivals, weddings and special family gatherings, this sweet treat is a true labour of love.

PREP TIME **45** mins | COOKING TIME **35–40** mins | MAKES **25-30** pcs

INGREDIENTS

500 g sugar
250 ml water
10 ml milk
250 ml ghee (divided)
35 g almonds, chopped
35 g cashew nuts, chopped
400 g coarse besan
2 g turmeric powder
2 g black cardamom powder
Pistachio powder, for garnish

METHOD

1. Add the sugar and water to a thick-bottom pan and heat on medium flame, stirring until the sugar dissolves completely. Once the syrup comes to a boil, add the milk. Skim off the Impurities that rise to the surface.
2. Continue boiling and keep stirring from the sides. The syrup will start crystallizing and turn grainy. At this stage, turn off the heat.
3. Stir continuously with a spatula as it cools. Keep stirring until it becomes a fine, powdery form known as tagar or boora. This will take 3–5 minutes. Allow it to cool down fully. Pass through a sieve for even texture. Store in an airtight jar.
4. Heat a heavy-bottom wok over medium heat, add 200 ml ghee, and let it melt. Lower the flame and add besan, and roast, stirring constantly.
5. Add the turmeric and break lumps while roasting. The mixture will loosen and then start binding. Roast for 25–30 minutes until the ghee separates.

Roasting determines the final flavour of the ladoo. Cook slowly over low heat, stirring continuously, until the besan turns aromatic and the ghee begins to separate. A brief sprinkling of water during roasting encourages a subtle granulation and deepens flavour. This step, though small, adds quiet complexity.

6. Add a dash of water and continue roasting on low heat until the moisture evaporates completely and the mixture becomes dry again. This will take about 2–3 minutes. The besan will look slightly lighter, fluffier and more aromatic. Repeat it one more time.
7. Add the nuts and cardamom powder. And gradually add in the remaining 50 ml ghee, 1 tbsp at a time, roasting for 2–3 minutes after each addition. Roast until the besan turns golden-brown and aromatic. Remove from heat and immediately transfer to a large plate.
8. Stir for 2–3 minutes so the mixture cools slightly and does not darken further. Let it cool to room temperature.
9. Mix in 200 g of the prepared boora / tagar. The sugar will absorb the ghee, and the mixture will bind.
10. Rest the mixture for 20–25 minutes. Shape into round ladoos. Garnish with pistachio powder.

picture on p.46

BESAN LADOO

GUJIA

GUJIA

CRESCENT-SHAPED PASTRY FILLED WITH KHOYA & NUTS

A beloved symbol of Holi and celebrations across North India, gujia is traditionally prepared in large batches with family. From shaping them to slow frying them, each step reflects care and celebration.

PREP TIME **30–35** mins (plus resting time)

COOKING TIME **20–25** mins

MAKES **12–15** pcs

INGREDIENTS

125 g all-purpose flour
40 ml melted ghee
50–60 ml water
20 g semolina
60 g khoya
25 g desiccated coconut
10 g pistachios, chopped
10 g cashew nuts, chopped
5 g Cuddapah almond (chironji)
30 g powdered sugar
10 g raisins, chopped
10 g almonds, slivered
2 g green cardamom powder
Ghee or neutral oil, for deep frying

METHOD

1. To prepare the dough for the gujia, combine the flour and ghee in a large mixing bowl. Rub between palms until the mix is crumbly.
2. Pour in the water little by little, and knead to make a firm dough. Cover with a damp cloth and set aside to rest for 20–30 minutes.
3. To prepare the filling, in a pan over low heat, roast semolina for 2–3 minutes, till light golden in colour. Remove from pan and set aside.
4. Add the khoya to the same pan, and sauté for 2–3 minutes until it turns slightly golden.
5. Add the desiccated coconut and chopped pistachios, cashew nuts and the chironji. Stir well to mix. Remove from heat and let it cool.
6. Now add the roasted semolina, powdered sugar, raisins and cardamom powder.

*

Resting the dough is essential. This allows the gluten to relax, making rolling and shaping easier. The filling must remain light and crumbly. Overcooking or excess moisture will make it dense and difficult to seal. Frying should be slow and even. Deep fry on medium-low heat to achieve a uniformly crisp, golden exterior. The gujia should feel light and crisp when done. This indicates the shell has cooked through fully.

7. Divide the prepared dough into small balls and roll into thin discs (10–12 cm). Press a ring cutter of 8 cm on top and press tightly to shape them into clean discs.
8. Take each disc and brush the edges with water. Place 2 tsp filling in the centre and fold into a half-moon shape, sealing edges firmly (you can twist edges, press with the fork or use a gujia mould).
9. Heat the ghee / oil on medium-low flame in a wok. Fry the gujia in batches for 6–8 minutes on each side, or until crisp and golden.
10. Use a slotted spoon and drain on paper towel-lined plate. Allow to cool completely before storing in an airtight container. They stay good for about a week.

picture on p.47

MOONG DAL HALWA

LENTIL DESSERT WITH GHEE & NUTS

Moong dal halwa is one of North India's most cherished winter desserts. The slow cooking is essential – it transforms humble lentils into a velvety, melt-in-the-mouth delicacy.

PREP TIME **30** mins (plus soaking time)

COOKING TIME **60** mins

SERVES **6–8**

INGREDIENTS

200 g split yellow mung beans (moong dal), skinned

200 ml ghee

10 g semolina

10 g gram flour (besan)

200 g sugar

200 ml water

Saffron, a few strands

2 g green cardamom powder

20 g pistachios, chopped

20 g almonds, chopped

20 g cashew nuts, chopped

75 g khoya, grated

METHOD

1. Wash and soak moong dal in water for 4–5 hours. Drain and add to a mixer-grinder and grind to a coarse paste. Ensure there is no excess water.
2. Heat the ghee in a heavy-bottom pan over medium heat. Add the semolina and besan. Reduce the heat to low and roast until golden brown and aromatic. Remove from heat and let cool down for 10 minutes.
3. Prepare a sugar syrup. In a saucepan on medium heat, combine the sugar and water. Cook until the sugar dissolves completely. Add the saffron and cardamom powder. Bring to a boil and remove from heat. Cover the pan and set aside.
4. Place the pan with the semolina and besan back on low-medium heat and add the ground moong dal. Roast for 25–30 minutes, stirring continuously until dal turns golden, grainy and releases a nutty aroma.
5. Now, carefully pour the hot sugar syrup into the roasted dal mixture, it will splutter. Stir continuously to avoid lumps.
6. Continue cooking on low heat for 10–12 minutes until the mixture thickens, ghee separates, and halwa leaves the sides of the pan.
7. Add the chopped nuts, and cook for 1 minute. Mix in grated khoya, cook for 2 minutes and take off the heat. Garnish with additional slivered pistachios and almonds. Serve warm.

PUNJABI PINNI

WHEAT FLOUR BALLS WITH GHEE & JAGGERY

Rooted in North Indian traditions, Punjabi pinni is a wholesome winter sweet. These energy-packed ladoos sustain families through the cold months, offering warmth and comfort in every bite.

PREP TIME **45–60** mins   COOKING TIME **45–50** mins   MAKES **25–30** pcs

INGREDIENTS

125 g poppy seeds
250 g wheat flour
250 g cashew nuts
625 g roasted chickpeas, with skin
1.625 L desi ghee (divided)
125 g edible gum (gond)
250 g fox nuts (makhana)
62 g fennel seed powder
62 g flame of the forest resin (kamar kas)
250 g almonds, coarsely chopped
250 g melon seeds
125 g raisins, halved
500 g flaxseed powder
25 g dry ginger powder
500 g jaggery powder
250 gm powdered sugar (boora)

METHOD

1. In a heavy-bottom pan on low-medium heat, dry roast the poppy seeds for 5 minutes. Set aside to cool. Once cool, add the poppy seeds to a mixer-grinder and grind to a powder. Keep aside.
2. In the same pan on low-medium heat, dry roast the wheat flour for 15–20 minutes, or until light golden and aromatic.
3. Crush the cashew nuts with a rolling pin. Add the roasted chickpeas to a mixer-grinder, and grind them into a medium fine powder. Keep aside.
4. Heat 150 ml ghee in a heavy-bottom pan and deep fry the edible gum till it puffs up. Remove with a strainer and crush roughly with mortar and pestle, while still warm.
5. Add 50 ml ghee to the pan, and fry the makhanas too. Take them off the heat and using a mortar and pestle, crush the makhana into a coarse powder.
6. Reduce the heat to low and add 200 ml ghee to the same pan. Add fennel seed powder and roast for 5–7 minutes.

The richness of Punjabi pinni lies in its composition. A balance of grains, nuts, seeds and ghee creates both structure and nourishment. Each ingredient is prepared individually. This ensures even roasting and allows every element to retain its distinct flavour and texture.

When fragrant, add kamar kas powder and roast for 2 minutes.

7. Now, add the almonds and the crushed cashew nuts. Add more ghee if required and roast for another 2–3 minutes.
8. Add the melon seeds. Roast for 3–4 minutes and add the raisins, flaxseed powder and dry ginger powder. Mix and continue to roast for 5–7 minutes. Add more ghee, if required.
9. Add the prepared poppy seed powder and combine well. Remove from heat and pour into a flat pan along with crushed makhanas and edible gum.
10. Add in the jaggery powder and mix while it is still hot. Using gloves, mix with hand, adding boora, roasted wheat flour and chickpea powder.
11. In a heavy-bottom pan over medium flame, heat the remaining ghee and add to the mix gradually. Rub with both hands, while it is still hot. You may not use all of the ghee here, just enough to shape into balls. While warm, shape the mixture into round or oval pinnis. Press gently to compact. Allow to cool completely at room temperature.
12. Store in an airtight container for 4–5 weeks.

picture on p.54

PUNJABI PINNI

CHURMA LADOO

CHURMA LADOO

CRUMBLED WHEAT FLOUR BALLS WITH GHEE & JAGGERY

Rooted in the culinary traditions of Rajasthan and Gujarat, churma ladoo is a celebration of grain, ghee and jaggery. It is traditionally prepared for weddings, temple offerings and family celebrations.

PREP TIME **45** mins | COOKING TIME **50–60** mins | MAKES **20–25** pcs

INGREDIENTS

500 g whole-wheat flour
50 g fine semolina
50 g gram flour (besan)
400 ml ghee (divided)
20 g raisins
15 g dried coconut, chopped
30 g almonds, chopped
30 g cashew nuts, chopped
20 g pistachios (chopped)
½ tsp green cardamom powder
1 pinch, freshly grated nutmeg
15 g rock sugar (mishri)
250 g jaggery, flaked

METHOD

1. In the large mixing bowl, add the whole-wheat flour, semolina, besan and 100 ml ghee. Rub with hands, and mix till it forms a rough ball when pressed together by hand.
2. Add 150–200 ml water and knead into a stiff dough.
3. Divide the dough into small portions and shape into thick muthiyas or oval discs.
4. Heat 200 ml ghee in a frying pan over medium heat. Reduce the heat to low and deep fry the muthiya for 10–15 minutes or until golden brown and crisp. Mash with a potato masher and let them cool completely.
5. In the same pan, fry the raisins in the same ghee till puffed. Set aside.
6. Add the chopped coconut pieces and fry for 2–3 minutes, or until they turn light brown.
7. Add the mashed muthiya in the mixer-grinder till evenly ground and set aside.
8. Place a frying pan on low heat. Add the ground muthiya and roast for about 10 minutes.

The foundation of churma ladoo lies in its grain. A blend of wheat flour, semolina and besan creates a balance of structure and lightness. The dough should remain firm. A stiff consistency ensures the muthiyas hold shape and fry evenly without absorbing excess ghee. And jaggery must be melted gently. Excess heat will harden it, affecting the final binding and texture.

9. Add the almonds, cashew nuts and pistachios and roast for 2 minutes. Transfer to a large bowl, and add cardamom powder and nutmeg. Add the raisins, coconut and mishri.
10. Heat the remaining 100 ml ghee in a pan over low heat. Add the jaggery and melt it on low heat (do not overheat). This will take 4–5 minutes.
11. Pour the melted jaggery and ghee mix over the dough and nuts mixture and mix well. Add little more melted ghee, as desired to make the ladoos.
12. While the mixture is warm but workable, grease hands with ghee and shape into ladoos. Let them set at room temperature.
13. Store in an airtight container for it to stay fresh for 10–12 days.

picture on p.55

PARIPPU PAYASAM

LENTIL & COCONUT MILK PUDDING

A treasured dessert from Kerala's culinary tradition, this payasam is an elegant harmony of lentils, jaggery and coconut milk, and reflects the simplicity of South Indian dessert-making.

PREP TIME **15** mins   COOKING TIME **30–35** mins   SERVES **4–5**

INGREDIENTS

220 g split yellow mung bean (moong dal)

875 ml water

300 g crushed jaggery

3 g green cardamom powder

2 g dry ginger powder

2 g roasted cumin powder

240 ml thick coconut milk

30 ml ghee

10 cashew nuts

20 g fresh coconut, thinly sliced

METHOD

1. Heat a wide pan over low heat, add the moong dal and dry roast for 10–15 minutes, or until they turn golden and aromatic. Take off the heat.
2. Add the roasted dal to a pressure cooker along with the water and place on medium heat. Pressure cook for 2–3 whistles. Allow the pressure to release naturally.
3. Alternatively, cook the dal in a heavy pan over low heat until soft and mushy. Use 1 litre water and keep the pan covered. Add some more water, if required. Lightly mash the cooked dal.
4. In another pan over low heat, melt the jaggery with 100 ml water. Strain to remove impurities and keep aside.
5. Transfer the cooked dal in a pan on medium heat. Add the jaggery syrup to the cooked dal. Stir and simmer for 5–7 minutes until well combined.
6. Add the cardamom, dry ginger and cumin powders. Stir well.
7. Lower the flame. Add the coconut milk and stir gently. Do not boil after adding thick coconut milk – just heat through. This will take 3–4 minutes.
8. Heat the ghee in a small pan over low heat. Fry the cashew nuts till golden. Remove from ghee and fry the coconut slices for 2 minutes or until crisp.
9. Pour the fried cashew nuts, coconut slices and ghee into the payasam. Mix gently. Serve warm.

SEMOLINA LADOO

SEMOLINA BALLS MADE WITH GHEE & NUTS

Creamy semolina is gently cooked, layered with toasted coconut and nuts, and sweetened to perfection, then shaped into bite-sized ladoos.

PREP TIME **15** mins COOKING TIME **25–30** mins MAKES **20–22** pcs

INGREDIENTS

200 g medium semolina
500 ml milk
80 g desiccated coconut
55 ml ghee (divided)
15 g slivered almonds
10 g chopped pistachios
1 g green cardamom powder
200 g powdered sugar

METHOD

1. Dry roast the semolina in a heavy pan on medium-low heat until very light golden and aromatic. This will take 20–25 minutes. Take off the heat.
2. Pour the roasted semolina gradually into room-temperature milk, stirring constantly to avoid lumps. Cover and keep aside for 15 minutes.
3. In a heavy pan on medium-low heat, dry roast the desiccated coconut lightly till it turns pale golden brown. This will take 7–8 minutes. Remove and keep aside.
4. Heat a heavy-bottom pan over low heat and add 30 ml ghee. Once the ghee has melted, add the soaked semolina and cook gently, stirring constantly so it does not catch at the bottom of the pan. Add 15 ml ghee and stir again, after 5 minutes, again add 10 ml ghee.
5. Continue cooking for 5–7 minutes, until the mixture thickens, begins to leave the sides of the pan, and looks almost dry, with no visible liquid remaining. Switch off the heat.
6. Add the almonds, pistachios and cardamom powder, and mix. Transfer to a bowl and leave to cool down completely.
7. Add the powdered sugar and mix with hands until it dissolves completely. Using your hands, shape them into ladoos.
8. Leave them to set at room temperature for about 20–30 minutes before storing in an airtight container. Store in an airtight container. It is best consumed within 4–5 days.

SOFT MYSORE PAK

GHEE-RICH GRAM FLOUR SQUARES

This Mysore pak is a luxurious take on the classic South Indian sweet, prized for its delicate crumb and melt-in-the-mouth texture. Best enjoyed fresh, this is a festive favourite.

PREP TIME **15** mins   COOKING TIME **20–25** mins   MAKES **16–18** pcs

INGREDIENTS

125 g gram flour (besan)
10 g all-purpose flour
250 ml ghee
125 ml water
250 g sugar
2 g green cardamom powder
1 pinch yellow food colour

METHOD

1. Sift both the gram flour and the all-purpose flour together well to remove any lumps.
2. Heat a heavy-bottom pan on medium heat and add the ghee. Once the ghee is hot, lower the flame to keep the ghee hot but not smoking. Add half the hot ghee to the flour and mix with a whisk.
3. In another heavy-bottom pan on medium heat, add the water along with the sugar, cardamom powder and yellow colour, and bring to a boil. Cook for 4–5 minutes, or until it lightly coats your finger and thumb when pressed (not a full string).
4. Lower the heat and add in the flour to the prepared sugar syrup, stirring quickly to avoid lumps. Begin adding the remaining hot ghee, 1–2 tbsp at a time, stirring continuously. The mixture will froth and bubble as the ghee gets absorbed.
5. Continue adding the ghee and cooking for 6–8 minutes, or until the mixture turns light and frothy, and starts to leave the sides of the pan. To test when done, take a small portion of dough in your hands and make a ball, if it doesn't stick to your fingers, it is ready.
6. Add in any remaining ghee, and immediately pour into a greased 6 x 6 inch tray, spread evenly, and tap to remove air gaps. Do not press too hard on top, otherwise all the air trapped will be lost.
7. Allow to cool for 10–15 minutes, then cut into squares. Do not wait too long or it will firm up more than desired.

MOTICHOOR LADOO PARFAIT

DELICATE BOONDI WITH GREEK YOGHURT & CREAM

*

This parfait is a playful fusion of traditional Indian mithai and modern dessert styling. Elegant yet comforting, this parfait is perfect for festive tables.

PREP TIME **35–40** mins | COOKING TIME **20–25** mins | SERVES **4–5**

INGREDIENTS

For the Motichoor

125 g gram flour (besan)

220 ml water (divided)

1 pinch baking soda

Oil or ghee, for deep frying

200 g sugar

1 pinch kesar yellow food colour

2 pinches red food colour

5 ml liquid glucose

10 g muskmelon seeds

For the Parfait

150 ml whipping cream

300 g Greek yoghurt

40 g powdered sugar

6–8 saffron strands,
soaked in 1 tbsp warm milk

2 g green cardamom powder

METHOD

1. To prepare the boondi, mix the besan and baking soda in a large mixing bowl. Gradually, add in 120 ml water, to form a thin, flowing batter.
2. Heat the oil / ghee in a deep pan on medium heat until very hot. Hold a perforated ladle (or a fine grater) over the oil and pour some batter. Tap lightly so tiny droplets fall into the oil.
3. Fry for 1–2 minutes, or until the boondi is crisp but not brown. Remove and place on a paper towel-lined plate to drain the excess oil. Repeat for all the batter.
4. To prepare the sugar syrup, add the sugar and the remaining 100 ml water in a pot on high heat. Bring to a boil and add the yellow and red food colour.
5. Reduce to low and simmer for 3–4 minutes, until the syrup reaches a one-string consistency (slightly sticky when pressed between the finger and thumb, but still light).
6. Turn the heat to medium and put the fried boondi and stir. Mix well until all the syrup is absorbed, and boondi looks soft, glossy and sticky. Remove from heat and set aside for 5 minutes. Add the liquid glucose and melon seeds, and mix. Set aside.

continued on p.66

200 g motichoor

25 g pistachios, chopped

20 g almonds, chopped

Dried rose petals, for garnish

2 tsp honey or rose syrup, optional, for drizzling

7. While still warm, take small portions (about 10–12 g each) and gently press between your palms to shape into mini ladoos for garnish. You will need 5 such ladoos for garnish. Set aside.
8. Leave the remaining motichoor loose for layering in the parfait.
9. To prepare the parfait, using a whisk, whip the cream for 2–3 minutes or until soft peaks form.
10. Fold in the Greek yoghurt, powdered sugar, saffron milk and cardamom powder. Mix gently until smooth and airy. Chill for 15 minutes.
11. In serving glasses, spoon some motichoor as the base layer. Add a spoonful of saffron–yoghurt cream mixture.
12. Sprinkle the chopped pistachios and almonds. Repeat layering until the glass is filled (usually 2 layers). Finish with a small ladoo on top. Garnish with rose petals, more nuts, and a light drizzle of honey or rose syrup. Chill for 30 minutes before serving for best flavour and texture.

PURAN POLI

LENTIL-STUFFED SWEET FLATBREADS

Traditionally prepared during Holi and Gudi Padwa, puran poli blurs the line between bread and dessert.

PREP TIME **35–40** min (plus soaking & resting time)

COOKING TIME **50–60** mins

MAKES **6** pcs

INGREDIENTS

For Puran (stuffing)

170 g Bengal gram lentil (chana dal)
500 ml water
3 g turmeric powder
15 ml ghee (divided)
125 g jaggery, grated
3 g cardamom powder
2 g nutmeg powder
2 g dry ginger powder

For Poli (dough)

120 g whole wheat flour
60 g all-purpose flour
2 g turmeric powder
2 g salt
30 ml oil
Water, as required, for kneading
Rice flour, for dusting
Ghee, for cooking

METHOD

1. To prepare the puran, wash and soak the chana dal for 3–4 hours. On medium heat, pressure cook the dal with 500 ml water, turmeric and 5 ml ghee for 3–4 whistles, until soft.
2. Drain excess water. In a mixer-grinder, grind the cooked dal with jaggery into a smooth paste.
3. In a heavy pan over medium heat, heat the remaining 10 ml ghee, and add the dal paste. Cook stirring continuously until the mixture thickens and leaves the sides of the pan.
4. Add the cardamom, nutmeg and ginger powder. Mix well and let it cool completely.
5. For the poli, in a mixing bowl, combine the whole-wheat flour, all-purpose flour, turmeric and salt. Gradually add water and knead into a soft, pliable dough. Add the oil and knead again to make a smooth dough. Cover and let it rest for at least 30 minutes.
6. Divide the dough and puran into 6 equal portions.
7. Roll out one dough ball into a small disc, place a puran ball in the centre. Seal by gathering the edges. Repeat for the remaining portions.
8. Gently roll out the ball into a flat, round disc, using rice flour for dusting, if needed. Repeat for the remaining dough balls.
9. Place a griddle on medium heat, cook the poli for 30–40 seconds, until light bubbles form and the surface looks slightly dry. Flip and apply ghee on one side and cook for 40–60 seconds until golden brown spots appear. Flip and cook for 20–30 seconds with a little more ghee. Serve hot.

BALUSHAHI

Flaky, deep-fried dough pastry

MALPUAS WITH RABRI

Fried pancakes with thickened milk

SHAHI TUKRA

Fried bread in saffron milk

CHENNA JALEBI

Syrup-soaked curdled milk spirals

GULAB JAMUN

Fried dough balls soaked in syrup

GULAB JAMUN CHEESECAKE

Cheesecake with gulab jamun filling

GHEVAR

Honeycomb disc soaked in sugar syrup

JALEBI

Crispy spirals soaked in syrup

GUR PARE

Crunchy, jaggery-coated dough bites

IMARTI

Thick, fried lentil spirals soaked in syrup

KHAJA

Layered crispy pastry

SYRUP-SOAKED & FRIED DELIGHTS

BALUSHAHI

FLAKY, DEEP-FRIED DOUGH PASTRY

✻

One of North India's most beloved festive sweets, balushahi's richness comes from slow frying in ghee and the careful balance of flour, fat, and gentle handling of the dough.

PREP TIME **30** mins (plus resting time)

COOKING TIME **35–40** mins

MAKES **18–20** pcs

INGREDIENTS

For the Dough

250 g all-purpose flour

2 g salt

2 g baking powder

2 g ammonium bicarbonate

80 ml ghee (for dough), warm
+ ghee or oil for deep frying

70 ml warm water

For the Sugar Syrup

300 g sugar

150 ml water

2–3 green cardamom pods, lightly crushed

Saffron, a few strands

2.5 ml lemon juice

Slivered pistachios, for garnish

METHOD

1. Sift the flour, salt, baking powder and ammonia together in a wide bowl.
2. Add the warm ghee to the flour and rub it with your fingertips until the mixture looks crumbly (like breadcrumbs).
3. Add the warm water gradually and gently bring the dough together. Do not knead – just mix lightly. The dough should be soft but not sticky. Cover and let it rest for 30 minutes.
4. Divide the dough into small balls, approximately 25 grams each. Gently flatten each ball and make a slight dent in the centre (like a doughnut, but not through).
5. Heat the ghee or oil in a deep pan on low to medium heat. It should be warm, not too hot. Frying on low heat is key for flaky layers. If the oil is too hot, they will remain raw on the inside.
6. Fry on low heat for 4–5 minutes on the first side without disturbing, then turn and fry for another 4–5 minutes until evenly golden and crisp. It takes 10–12 minutes per batch. Remove and drain on paper.

The character of balushahi lies in its layers. A delicate balance of flour and ghee creates a structure that is crisp outside and flaky within. The dough should be handled lightly. Minimal mixing ensures the layers remain distinct and prevents a dense texture.

Frying determines the texture. Cook slowly over low heat so the layers form gradually and the interior cooks through evenly. The balushahi should rise gently and turn evenly golden.

7. To make the sugar syrup, combine the sugar and water in a pan and bring to boil on high heat. When it comes to a boil, add the crushed cardamom pods and a few saffron strands.
8. Cook until the syrup reaches one-thread consistency. When checked with a thermometer, the temperature should be 105°C. Add in the lemon juice to prevent crystallization. Remove from heat.
9. Soak the hot fried balushahi in batches in warm sugar syrup for 2–3 minutes, till the syrup seeps inside. Remove and place on a plate. Garnish with pistachios.

picture on p.72

BALUSHAHI

MALPUAS WITH RABRI

MALPUAS WITH RABRI

FRIED PANCAKES WITH THICKENED MILK

Lightly crisp at the edges and soft at the centre, the fennel- and cardamom-scented malpuas absorb just enough fragrant sugar syrup to turn irresistibly juicy.

PREP TIME **30** mins | COOKING TIME **45** mins | SERVES **4–6**

INGREDIENTS

For the Rabri

1 L full-fat milk

2 white bread slices

100 g sugar

1 g green cardamom powder

Saffron, a few strands

3 ml pandanus (kewra) water

For the Sugar Syrup

250 g caster sugar

180 ml water

4 green cardamom pods, lightly crushed

Saffron, a few strands

5 ml lemon juice

For the Malpuas

150 g all-purpose flour

50 g milk powder

5 g fennel seeds, lightly crushed

METHOD

1. For the rabri, pour the milk in a heavy-bottom pan and heat on high flame. Once the milk comes to a boil, reduce to medium heat and cook until it reduces to half the quantity. This will take 30–35 minutes.
2. Remove the edges of the bread slices and crumble. Add the crumbled bread to the milk. Stir well, so that the bread absorbs the milk and thickens.
3. Add the sugar, cardamom powder and saffron. Cook for 10–12 minutes while stirring, until the mixture becomes thick and creamy. Finish by adding kewra water.
4. To make the sugar syrup, add the sugar and water to a saucepan and bring to a boil on high heat.
5. Add the cardamom pods and saffron strands. Turn the heat to low and let simmer for 5–6 minutes until it reaches a light syrup consistency. To test if the syrup is ready, dip a spatula into it, then cool for a minute. Squish a drop between index finger and thumb, then pull your fingers apart – the syrup should form a single thread. Alternatively, a digital or sugar thermometer should read 105°C.

15 g caster sugar

1 g green cardamom powder

1 pinch baking powder

220 ml milk, as needed

400 ml ghee, for frying

30 g chopped nuts (almonds, pistachios, cashew nuts)

6. Add the lemon juice to prevent crystallization. Keep warm on the lowest heat.
7. To make the malpua batter, combine the flour, milk powder, fennel seeds, sugar, cardamom and baking powder in a bowl.
8. Slowly add 180–220 ml milk to form a smooth, thick, pancake-like batter. It should coat the back of a spoon, not runny. Rest the batter for 20–30 minutes.
9. To fry the malpuas, heat the ghee in a shallow frying pan over medium heat.
10. Pour a small ladleful of batter into the hot oil. It will spread into a small pancake.
11. Fry for 1½–2 minutes on one side, or until golden brown at the edges, then flip and cook the other side for 1 minute.
12. Drain briefly on kitchen paper, then dip each hot malpua into the warm sugar syrup for 30–40 seconds. Remove and set aside.
13. Spread some rabri on the serving platter. Put a few malpuas on top. Sprinkle with chopped nuts. Serve warm.

picture on p.73

SHAHI TUKRA

FRIED BREAD IN SAFFRON MILK & TOPPED WITH NUTS

Shahi tukra, meaning 'royal piece' is a decadent Mughlai dessert that transforms simple bread into an opulent treat.

PREP TIME **20** mins

COOKING TIME **45–50** mins

SERVES **8–10**

INGREDIENTS

For the Fried Bread

12 white bread slices

200 ml ghee

1 L milk

Saffron, a few strands

200 g caster sugar

10 g dried rose petals

1 pinch green cardamom powder

For the Rabri

1 L milk

Saffron, a few strands

100 g sugar

2 g green cardamom powder

30 g slivered pistachios, for garnish

30 g slivered almonds, for garnish

Silver leaf, for garnish

METHOD

1. Remove the brown edges from the bread slices and cut into neat triangles. Remove the pointed edges, otherwise it tends to burn while frying.
2. Heat the ghee in a shallow pan and deep fry the bread over low heat for 2–3 minutes, or until golden and crisp. Drain and keep aside.
3. To prepare the milk for soaking, bring the milk to a boil in a wide pan on high heat. Stir the milk for 8–10 minutes, or until it reduces a bit.
4. Add in a few strands of saffron and cook further for 12–15 minutes, until it reduces to half. Stir in the caster sugar, dried rose petals and a pinch of cardamom powder.
5. Reduce the heat to low, and add the fried bread triangles; do not stir. When the bread is very soft, but not breaking, remove to individual platters, along with a few spoons of milk.
6. To prepare the rabri, add the milk in the same pan with leftover milk. Bring to a boil, stirring continuously and cook for 30–35 minutes, or until the milk is reduced to half.
7. Add the saffron, sugar and cardamom powder. Cook on low heat for 8–10 minutes, until thick. Remove from heat and cool to room temperature.
8. Pour a ladleful of rabri over the bread and garnish with slivered pistachios, almonds and silver leaf.

CHENNA JALEBI

SYRUP-SOAKED CURDLED-MILK SPIRALS

Popular in eastern and northern India, chenna jalebi reflects the artistry of halwai kitchens, where patience, precise temperatures and careful kneading transform simple milk into a celebration sweet.

PREP TIME **45** mins (plus time for draining chenna)

COOKING TIME **30–35** mins

MAKES **20–25** pcs

INGREDIENTS

For the Chenna

1 L full cream milk

1 g citric acid crystals

10 g fine semolina

10 g all-purpose flour

5 g cornflour

5 g baking powder

1 pinch baking soda

500 ml ghee (or **250 ml** ghee + **250 ml** refined oil, for frying)

For the Sugar Syrup

500 g sugar

250 ml water

2 green cardamom pods, lightly crushed

Saffron, a few strands

3 ml pandanus (kewra) water

METHOD

1. In a small bowl, dilute the citric acid crystals in 100 ml water. Set aside.
2. In a pan over medium heat, bring the milk to a boil, switch off flame, and cool for 2 minutes. Add the diluted citric acid gradually, and stir until the milk curdles. You may not need all of the citric acid solution.
3. Strain through a muslin cloth, and rinse with cold water to remove sourness. Knot the cloth and hang for 30 minutes to drain excess water.
4. Transfer the chenna to a plate and knead with the heel of your palm until soft and smooth. Kneading chenna properly is key to smooth jalebis.
5. Add the semolina, flour, cornflour, baking powder and baking soda to the kneaded chenna. Knead until everything is well mixed and you have a smooth, pliable dough.
6. Add the dough in a piping bag with a closed star tip nozzle.
7. To prepare the sugar syrup, heat the sugar and water in a pan on low heat first so the sugar dissolves evenly, then increase

The essence of chenna jalebi lies in the chenna. Freshly curdled milk must be soft, moist and free of excess whey. Kneading determines the final texture. Work the chenna until smooth and pliable, without any graininess. The dough should feel light and cohesive. This ensures the jalebis hold shape while remaining soft within.

to medium and cook until it reaches 105°C. The syrup should be thick and just about one-string consistency.

8. Add the cardamom, saffron and kewra water. Reduce the heat to low and keep the sugar syrup warm.
9. To fry the jalebi, heat the ghee on medium-low heat. First pipe the jalebi in a spiral, on your hand, then gently place the shaped chenna spirals into the ghee. Fry for 3–4 minutes on low flame until they turn golden and crisp. Avoid high heat, as they may break.
10. Remove the fried jalebis and immediately immerse in the warm sugar syrup. Always soak while syrup is warm, not cold. Let them soak for at least 20–25 minutes. Drain and serve warm or at room temperature.

picture on p.80

CHENNA JALEBI

GULAB JAMUN

GULAB JAMUN

FRIED DOUGH BALLS SOAKED IN SYRUP

Few Indian sweets are as universally loved as gulab jamun. This version, made with a blend of khoya and paneer, yields tender jamuns with a rich flavour and a melt-in-the-mouth texture.

PREP TIME **25–30** mins (plus soaking time)

COOKING TIME **20–25** mins

SERVES **10–12**

INGREDIENTS

For the dough

500 g khoya, softened
150 g paneer
100 g all-purpose flour
2 g green cardamom powder
2 g baking powder
Ghee, for deep frying

For the sugar syrup

1.5 kg sugar
800 ml water
4 green cardamom pods
Saffron, a few strands

METHOD

1. To prepare the gulab jamun dough, grate the khoya and paneer into a large mixing bowl.
2. Add the all-purpose flour, baking powder and cardamom powder. Mix gently and knead into a smooth, soft dough. Cover and keep aside for 15 minutes.
3. Meanwhile, to prepare the sugar syrup, in a deep pan over medium flame, combine the sugar and water. Heat until the sugar dissolves completely.
4. Add the cardamom pods and saffron. Let it simmer for 5–7 minutes, turn off the heat and keep aside.
5. Once the dough is rested, take a portion of dough and knead a little on the countertop. Roll into a thick rope and divide the dough into 18–20 g small, smooth balls or roll them into a cylindrical shape, ensuring there are no cracks. Place them in a rimless plate, as will fit in the pan for frying. Repeat with rest of the mix.

The sugar syrup should be light and aromatic. A thin consistency allows it to soak deeply without becoming heavy. Both syrup and jamuns should be warm during soaking. This ensures proper absorption and a soft, juicy texture. Allow sufficient soaking time. This helps the syrup penetrate fully to the centre.

6. Heat the ghee in a wok or a deep-frying pan on low-medium flame. When it is hot enough, work in batches and carefully slide the dough balls, from the plate. Remove the wok from the heat, but continue stirring till the balls start to float on top.
7. Meanwhile, place the sugar syrup on low heat. And once the syrup is warm, set aside.
8. Once the ghee in the wok starts turning cold, place it back on the flame again and using a frying ladle, stir in the centre, so that the jamuns are rotating all the time. Fry for 6–8 minutes, or until deep golden brown all over.
9. Remove the gulab jamuns and place on a kitchen paper-lined tray to drain the excess ghee. Immediately drop the fried gulab jamuns into the warm sugar syrup. Let them soak for at least 2–3 hours. They will absorb the syrup and become soft and juicy.
10. Serve warm, allowing the jamuns to be soft, aromatic and fully infused with syrup. They can also be served at room temperature, where the texture firms up slightly and the sweetness feels more settled.

picture on p.81

GULAB JAMUN CHEESECAKE

CHEESECAKE WITH GULAB JAMUN FILLING

This dessert bridges tradition and modern patisserie, making it ideal for festive celebrations, dinner parties and special occasions when you want to serve something both familiar and surprising.

PREP TIME **35** min (plus chilling time)

COOKING TIME **55–60** min

SERVES **8–10**

INGREDIENTS

For the Base

200 g digestive biscuits

100 g unsalted butter (melted)

15 g chopped pistachios, for garnish

A few dried rose petals, for garnish

Saffron, a few strands, for garnish

For the Cheesecake Filling

400 g cream cheese, room temperature

150 g Greek yoghurt / hung curd

120 g caster sugar

200 ml fresh cream

20 g cornflour

5 ml rose water

2 g green cardamom powder

10–12 saffron strands, soaked in 1 tbsp warm milk

10–12 pieces of small gulab jamuns or 6 large gulab jamuns (store-bought or homemade, drained from syrup)

METHOD

1. To prepare the base, crush the biscuits into fine crumbs with a rolling pin. Place this in a mixing bowl and add the melted butter and mix – the biscuit mix should be sandy in texture.
2. Press the biscuit mix evenly into the bottom of a 20 cm springform pan. Chill in the fridge for 20 minutes to set.
3. To prepare the cheesecake filling, whisk together the cream cheese, Greek yoghurt or hung curd and caster sugar in a large bowl until smooth. Fold in the fresh cream, cornflour, rose water, cardamom powder and the saffron milk. Mix until well combined, but do not over-beat.
4. To assemble the cheesecake, pour half of the cheesecake filling over the biscuit base. Place the gulab jamuns (cut in half if using large ones), evenly across the filling. Pour the remaining filling over and smooth the top.
5. Preheat the oven to 160°C. Wrap the base of the pan with foil and place it in a larger tray. Pour hot water into the tray until it reaches halfway up the sides of the pan. Bake for 55–60 minutes, until the edges are set but the centre remains slightly wobbly.
6. Turn off the oven, leave the cheesecake inside with the door slightly open for 30 minutes. Remove and cool completely at room temperature. Refrigerate for at least 6 hours or overnight. Top with the chopped pistachios, rose petals and a few saffron strands. Slice and serve chilled.

GHEVAR

HONEYCOMB DISC SOAKED IN SUGAR SYRUP

Ghevar is one of Rajasthan's most iconic sweets, prized for its delicate honeycomb texture and luxurious finish. It is traditionally prepared for festivals such as Teej and Raksha Bandhan.

PREP TIME **45–50** mins COOKING TIME **30–35** mins SERVES **6–8**

INGREDIENTS

For the Batter

25 ml ghee
50 g ice
125 g all-purpose flour
25 g gram flour (besan)
325 ml water (divided)
Oil, or ghee for deep-frying
Slivered pistachios, for garnish
Dried rose petals, for garnish
Saffron, a few strands, for garnish

For the Sugar Syrup

750 g sugar
600 ml water (divided)
2 green cardamoms, crushed
2.5 ml rose water

For the Milk Soak

1.25 L milk
0.5 ml citric acid
Green cardamom powder, a pinch
Saffron, a few strands

METHOD

1. To make the batter, heat the ghee in a small pan over medium heat and transfer to a large wide pan. Add the ice, and mix with hand in a clockwise motion, till the ghee solidifies, and turns white in colour.
2. Remove the ice, and continue mixing with your hand for 2–3 minutes, or until smooth. Remove the excess water and continue mixing for 4–5 minutes, or until it acquires a soft, butter-like consistency; this step is very important.
3. In a large bowl, mix the all-purpose flour and gram flour.
4. Take 50 ml water in a mixing bowl, add a small quantity of flour and mix. Repeat this process till all the flour and water is used. This ensures that the batter is lump free. The batter should be slightly thinner than pancake batter. Allow the batter to rest for 15–30 minutes.
5. Heat the oil or ghee in a flat medium-deep pan to 170–180°C. To test it without a thermometer, drop a few drops of batter into the oil. The batter should immediately rise to the surface and begin to spread into a lacy pattern. If it sinks and stays at the bottom, the oil is not hot enough. Place one or two metal rings (depending on the size of ghevar desired) in the oil. The oil should cover till the half height of the ring.
6. For the sugar syrup, combine the sugar and 500 ml water. Bring to a boil in a large saucepan over medium heat. After 2 minutes, add the remaining water and remove the scum

The pouring technique is crucial for the shape of the ghevar. A thin stream from height allows the batter to disperse and form its lacy pattern. Temperature control is critical. The fat must remain steady – too hot and the structure closes, too cool and it will not set. The central hole must remain open. This allows layering and ensures even cooking throughout.

from top. Boil till it is shiny, switch off before it reaches one-string consistency.

7. Add the crushed cardamom and rose water and keep warm.
8. Put some batter in a squeezable sauce bottle and pour in a thin stream in batches into hot oil in the centre of the ring from a height, forming circular lacy layers. If the oil gets too hot, add a ladle of oil. Ensure there is a hole in the centre for pouring the batter, if it gets closed, use a knife to open it.
9. The ghevar shouldn't stick on the sides. Fry for 4–5 minutes, or until golden and crisp, till it stops bubbling on top.
10. Stick a knife in the centre, and hold it at an angle and remove from the oil. Place on a wire rack and pour the syrup on top. Leave it for 5 minutes to drain the excess syrup. Repeat with the rest of the batter.
11. To prepare the milk for the soak, boil the milk in a heavy-bottom pan on medium heat for 35–45 minutes till reduced to half, stirring occasionally.
12. Add the citric acid and increase the heat, so that it becomes granular in texture. Keep stirring till it is thick. Add cardamom powder and saffron.
13. Spread the thickened milk generously over the cooled ghevar for a richer taste. Garnish with the pistachios, rose petals and saffron strands.

picture on p.88

GHEVAR

JALEBI

JALEBI

CRISPY SPIRALS SOAKED IN SUGAR SYRUP

Crisp on the outside, syrupy within and delicately tangy from natural fermentation, jalebi is one of India's most iconic sweets.

PREP TIME **30** mins
(plus soaking & dough preparation)

COOKING TIME **45–50** mins

SERVES **8–10**

INGREDIENTS

For the Batter

400 g all-purpose flour, divided

500 ml water

1 pinch turmeric

Ghee or neutral oil, for frying

Pistachios, slivered, for garnish

For the Sugar Syrup

500 g sugar

250 ml water

3 ml lemon juice

2 green cardamom pods, lightly crushed

Saffron, a few strands

5 ml rose water

METHOD

1. In a clean bowl, mix 200 gm all-purpose flour and 220–250 ml water to make a flowing batter. Add water little by little to make a lump-free, thick, yet pourable batter. Beat with your hand in one direction, till fluffy and smooth.
2. Cover loosely and leave it in a warm place for 24 hours (in cooler weather, up to 36 hours). These jalebis will have a more complex, slightly tangy flavour.
3. The batter should develop a light sour aroma and small bubbles – this means it's fermented naturally. Sift the remaining 200 gm flour over the batter and mix with the remaining water gradually to make thick flowing batter, and again beat with your hand in one direction.
4. To make the sugar syrup, heat the sugar and water in a pan and bring to a boil. Start on low heat first to dissolve the sugar, stirring continuously. Increase the heat and simmer till it reaches one-string consistency. At this stage, the temperature should be 105°C. Add the lemon juice, cardamom, saffron and rose water. Keep warm (not hot).

The character of jalebi is defined by fermentation. A naturally fermented batter develops its signature tang and lightness. The batter should be smooth and aerated. Beating in one direction incorporates air and improves texture. Piping requires steadiness. Even spirals ensure uniform cooking and structure. Frying should be even and unhurried. Allow the jalebis to set before turning to maintain shape.

5. Heat the ghee / oil in a wide flat pan over medium heat.
6. Fill the fermented batter in a piping bag, or a cloth with a hole, or a squeeze bottle. Pipe spirals directly into hot oil. The oil should be hot enough that when you pipe the jalebi, it should come up immediately.
7. Fry on medium heat until golden and crisp. Do not turn the side for first 2–3 minutes. Fry each jalebi for 10–12 minutes.
8. Transfer the fried jalebis immediately to the warm sugar syrup. Let soak for 20–30 seconds, then lift out. Sprinkle with pistachios and serve with rabri or vanilla ice cream.

picture on p.89

GUR PARE

CRUNCHY, JAGGERY-COATED DOUGH BITES

Often prepared during winters and festive seasons, gur pare is a favourite in home kitchens and sweet shops alike, enjoyed with afternoon tea or shared during celebrations.

PREP TIME **25–30** mins COOKING TIME **20–25** mins MAKES **20-25** pcs

INGREDIENTS

For the Dough

250 g all-purpose flour

2 g salt

1 pinch baking powder

1 pinch baking soda

75 ml ghee

80–100 ml water (add more if required)

Oil, for frying

For the Jaggery Syrup

125 g jaggery, crushed

125 g sugar

125 ml water

3.5 g fennel seeds

2 g dry ginger powder

1 pinch baking soda

10 ml ghee

METHOD

1. To prepare the dough, combine the flour, salt, baking powder and baking soda in a large bowl. Add the ghee and rub into the flour until it resembles breadcrumbs. Gradually add the water and knead into a stiff and rough dough. Cover and rest for 15–20 minutes.
2. Roll out the dough into a 1-cm-thick rectangle without smoothening it out. Cut into rectangular 2 x 6 cm sized pieces.
3. Heat the oil in a heavy-bottom wok on low heat. Add as many pare as will fit in the pan. Don't stir, just tap the strainer on top a few times.
4. Fry for 3–4 minutes on the first side, then turn gently and fry for another 2–3 minutes on low heat, until they turn golden and crisp. Before removing the pare, increase the heat to high for 1 minute. Remove and drain on paper towels.
5. For the jaggery syrup, heat the jaggery, sugar and water in a pot over low heat. Cook for 8–10 minutes, or until thick and sticky, just before it reaches one-string consistency.
6. Add the fennel, ginger powder and the baking soda and give it a stir.
7. Remove from heat and immediately add the fried pare to the syrup and toss quickly to coat. Add 10 ml ghee and stir gently, till jaggery syrup becomes dry. Spread on a greased plate and separate pieces before they harden. Once cool, store in an airtight container.

IMARTI

THICK, FRIED LENTIL SPIRALS SOAKED IN SYRUP

Made from fermented urad dal batter and fried in ghee, imarti offers a depth of flavour and lightness that sets it apart from its close cousin, jalebi.

PREP TIME **20** mins
(plus soaking & fermentation time)

COOKING TIME **30** mins

SERVES **8–10**

INGREDIENTS

For the Batter

200 g split black gram without skin (urad dal)

100–120 ml water

8–10 g cornflour

1 pinch orange-red food colour

500 ml ghee, for deep frying

20 g almonds, slivered

For the Sugar Syrup

400 g sugar

200 ml water

2 g green cardamom powder

Saffron, a few strands

3 ml lemon juice

METHOD

1. Wash and soak the urad dal in water for 6 hours or overnight.
2. Drain the dal completely and grind to a smooth, thick, fluffy batter using 100–120 ml water. Batter should be light and airy. Mix in cornflour and food colour. Set aside for 30–60 minutes for slight fermentation.
3. To prepare the sugar syrup, add the sugar and water to a pan on high heat. Boil for 6–8 minutes till it reaches one-string consistency. The temperature at this stage should be 105°C.
4. Add the cardamom powder, saffron and lemon juice, and give it a stir. Turn the heat to low and keep the syrup warm.
5. Heat the ghee in a flat, wide pan on medium heat.
6. Fill the batter into a piping bag or cloth with a small round hole. Pipe the batter in concentric rings with small loops around (like a flower shape) into the hot ghee.
7. Fry on medium heat for 5–6 minutes on each side, or until golden and crisp.
8. Remove the fried imartis and immediately dip into warm sugar syrup. Let them soak for 30–40 seconds only. Lift and place on a plate to set. Garnish with almonds and serve.

KHAJA

LAYERED, CRISPY PASTRY

Khaja is a classic festive sweet that showcases the beauty of careful layering and slow frying.

PREP TIME **30** mins   COOKING TIME **40–50** mins   MAKES **8–10** pcs

INGREDIENTS

For the Dough

190 g all-purpose flour

3 g salt

70 ml ghee

70–80 ml water, as required

For the Sugar Syrup

300 g sugar

180 ml water

For Frying and Rolling

Oil, for deep frying

All-purpose flour, as required (for dusting and layering)

Ghee, as required (for layering the folds while rolling)

METHOD

1. In a mixing bowl, add the all-purpose flour, salt and 40 ml ghee. Rub with your fingertips until the mixture is crumbly. Add the water little by little, and knead into a firm but smooth dough. Cover and rest for 20–30 minutes.
2. Divide the dough into four equal portions. Roll each into thin discs. With the remaining ghee, spread about 1–1½ tsp ghee in a thin layer over one disc, dust lightly with flour, place another disc on top. Repeat with all layers.
3. Cut all the four edges of the round stack to make into a square, then roll the stack tightly, from the side farthest to you, into a log. Seal the edges with water. Cut the log into 2-cm pieces. Flatten each piece lightly in the centre and then press into a rectangle with a small rolling pin. Finish rolling all the pieces.
4. To prepare the sugar syrup, heat the sugar and water in a pan on medium heat. Boil it until it just reaches one-string consistency, if checked with a digital thermometer, the temperature should be 105°C. Reduce the heat to low and keep warm.
5. Heat the oil in a heavy-bottom wide pan on medium flame. Add as many khajas as will fit in the pan, and then switch off the heat. When the khajas start floating in the oil, turn on the heat. Fry the khajas in batches on low–medium heat for 8–10 minutes, or until golden brown and crisp.
6. Immediately dip hot khajas into warm sugar syrup for 2 minutes. Remove and place on a greased plate. Serve.

PHIRNI

Creamy rice pudding with milk & nuts

KHEER

Creamy rice pudding

RED AVAL PAYASAM

Rice flakes cooked in milk & sugar

CHAKKARA PONGAL

Rice & moong dal pudding

ZAFRANI SEMOLINA HALWA

Saffron-infused semolina pudding

RICE & GRAIN-BASED SWEETS

PHIRNI

CREAMY RICE PUDDING WITH MILK & NUTS

Delicately thick and wonderfully soothing, phirni is a classic North Indian rice pudding traditionally set in earthen bowls and served chilled.

PREP TIME **25** mins
(plus soaking time)

COOKING TIME **35–40** mins

SERVES **4–5**

INGREDIENTS

60 g rice

1 L full-fat milk (divided)

50 g almonds

Saffron, a few strands
+ a few strands for garnish

2 g green cardamom powder

110 g sugar

Almonds, slivered, for garnish

METHOD

1. Soak the terracotta or earthenware pots, if using, in water for a few hours. Drain and let them dry. Skip this step if you are using bowls to serve this.
2. Wash the rice thoroughly and soak in water for 30 minutes. Drain and grind with 50 ml milk on pulse mode until smooth. Set aside.
3. Soak the almonds in warm water for 30 minutes and peel them. Grind the peeled almonds with 50 ml milk to a smooth paste.
4. Heat the remaining 900 ml milk in a heavy-bottom pan over low heat. Bring to a gentle boil, stirring occasionally.
5. Add the almond paste to the boiling milk, stirring continuously. Simmer on low heat for 5–10 minutes.
6. Add the rice paste and bring to a quick boil. Stir occasionally to make sure it doesn't burn at the bottom.
7. Add the saffron and cook on medium-low heat till it becomes thick and creamy, and the rice is cooked. This should take 12–15 minutes.
8. Add the cardamom powder along with sugar. Stir well and cook for 5 minutes.
9. Pour into serving bowls and let cool to room temperature. Refrigerate for 1–2 hours. Garnish with slivered almonds and a few saffron strands.

KHEER

CREAMY RICE PUDDING

Whether served warm on a festive evening or chilled on a summer afternoon, this classic is the very essence of comfort and celebration.

PREP TIME **20** mins (plus soaking time)

COOKING TIME **50–60** mins

SERVES **6–8**

INGREDIENTS

150 g short-grain rice

30 g almonds

2 L milk

2 g green cardamom powder

20 g raisins

20 g Cuddapah almond (chironji)

200 g sugar

2 pinches saffron (soaked in 1 tbsp warm milk)

METHOD

1. Rinse the rice well and soak for 30 minutes. Drain.
2. Soak the almonds in hot water for 15 minutes. Peel and cut into slivers. Set aside.
3. In a heavy-bottom pan, bring the milk to a boil over high heat. Lower the flame and let it simmer, stirring occasionally so it doesn't stick to the bottom of the pan.
4. Add the soaked rice to the simmering milk. Cook on low heat, stirring often, until rice turns soft and the milk reduces and thickens. This should take about 35–40 minutes.
5. Add the cardamom powder, sliced almonds, raisins and chironji.
6. Stir in the sugar and saffron-infused milk. Continue cooking for 10 minutes until well-blended.
7. Cook for another 5 minutes. Remove from heat and stir for 5–10 minutes. Serve warm or chilled, garnished with a few extra saffron strands and nuts, if you like.

RED AVAL PAYASAM

RICE FLAKES COOKED IN MILK & SUGAR

A comforting South Indian dessert made with thick red rice flakes, jaggery and milk. Enriched with ghee, it is finished with cashew nuts and plump raisins for texture and richness.

PREP TIME **10** mins COOKING TIME **20** mins SERVES **3–4**

INGREDIENTS

175 g jaggery

250 ml water

30 ml ghee (divided)

75 g red rice flakes (aval / poha), thicker variety

750 ml hot milk

5 g green cardamom powder

2 g dry ginger powder

12 cashew nuts

15 raisins

METHOD

1. Heat the jaggery with 250 ml water in a heavy-bottom pan over medium heat, stirring occasionally until the jaggery has completely dissolved. This should take about 4–5 minutes.
2. Once the jaggery is dissolved, let the mixture simmer for a further 3–4 minutes, until slightly thickened. The syrup should look smooth and glossy, with the consistency of thin maple syrup – not too thick or sticky. Strain to remove impurities and keep aside.
3. Heat 15 g ghee in a pan over medium heat. Once the ghee is hot, add the aval and roast on low heat for 2–3 minutes, until lightly crisp and aromatic.
4. Add the hot milk, stir and simmer for 8–10 minutes, until creamy and the flakes soften.
5. Now pour the jaggery syrup into the aval. Cook on low flame for 5 minutes.
6. Remove from heat and stir in the cardamom powder and ginger powder. Mix well.
7. For the garnish, heat the remaining ghee in another pan. And add the cashew nuts and raisins. They are ready when the cashew nuts turn golden and the raisins puff up. Add them along with the ghee to the payasam. Stir well and serve warm.

CHAKKARA PONGAL

RICE & MOONG DAL PUDDING

This celebratory dish from South India is prepared especially during harvest festivals and as temple offering. The finishing touch of ghee-fried coconut, cashews and raisins adds richness and texture.

PREP TIME **20** mins
(plus soaking time)

COOKING TIME **30** mins

SERVES **6–8**

INGREDIENTS

200 g raw rice

50 g split yellow mung bean (moong dal)

400 g jaggery

685 ml water (divided)

1 pinch salt

100 ml ghee (divided)

3 g cardamom powder

40 g coconut, thinly sliced

30 g cashew nuts

15 g raisins

METHOD

1. Combine the rice and moong dal together in a bowl. Wash thoroughly and soak in water for 2 hours, and drain.
2. In a pan on low heat, melt the jaggery with 60 ml water. Remove from heat and strain to remove impurities.
3. In a pressure cooker over medium heat, add the rice and dal with 625 ml water and a pinch of salt. Cook for 2–3 whistles. The mixture should be soft, but not completely mushy.
4. Release the pressure, open the lid and put it back on low heat. While it is hot, add 30 g ghee, and stir gently to get a smooth and shiny texture.
5. Stir the jaggery syrup into the cooked rice-dal mixture. Add the cardamom powder and 30 g ghee. Stir continuously on high heat until well combined and slightly thickened, no more than 5 minutes.
6. Heat the remaining 40 g ghee in a separate pan. Add the coconut slices and cashew nuts and fry for 2 minutes, or until they turn light brown. Add the raisins and fry until plump. Add them along with the ghee to the pongal. Mix well to combine.
7. When dropped from the spoon, the pongal should fall smoothly. Serve warm.

ZAFRANI SEMOLINA HALWA

SAFFRON-INFUSED SEMOLINA PUDDING

This is a celebration dessert traditionally prepared in community kitchens and for feasts. It is best enjoyed warm, when its aroma, richness and golden glow are at their most irresistible.

PREP TIME **20** mins COOKING TIME **45–50** mins SERVES **8–10**

INGREDIENTS

1 kg sugar

3 L water

Saffron, a few strands

1 L ghee

1 kg semolina

200 g cashew nuts

200 g almonds

150 g pistachios

METHOD

1. In a large pan, combine the sugar and water. Heat on low flame for 6–8 minutes, until the sugar dissolves completely. Bring to a boil, add the saffron strands and simmer for 2–3 minutes. Keep the syrup warm on low heat.
2. In a heavy-bottom pan over medium heat, heat the ghee. Once the ghee is hot, add the semolina and roast on medium-low heat for 18–22 minutes, or until it turns golden brown and aromatic.
3. Roughly chop the cashew nuts, almonds and pistachios, and add to the semolina mix. Roast for 2 minutes.
4. Then, carefully pour half the warm sugar syrup into the roasted semolina while stirring continuously. Be careful with this, as it will splutter. Cook for 5–6 minutes on medium heat, allowing the semolina to absorb the liquid.
5. Add the remaining syrup and cook on medium-high heat for 6–8 minutes, stirring continuously, until the semolina fully absorbs the syrup and thickens to a soft, glossy mass.
6. Switch off the heat, cover with a lid, and allow it to rest for 15 minutes.
7. Remove the cover and stir again until the halwa reaches a soft, cohesive consistency. Serve warm, garnished with extra nuts, if desired.

MANGO KULFI
Rich, frozen mango ice cream

AAMRAS
Velvety mango pulp delight

BANANA HALWA
Rich, caramelized banana pudding

CARROT HALWA
Velvety, slow-cooked carrot pudding

JACKFRUIT HALWA
Rich, sticky jackfruit fudge

TENDER COCONUT PAYASAM
Delicate, creamy coconut pudding

CASHEW NUT BARFI
Rich cashew nut fudge

PISTACHIO & COCONUT SQUARES
No-bake pistachio & coconut treats

FRUIT & NUT-BASED SWEETS

MANGO KULFI

RICH, FROZEN MANGO ICE CREAM

Served straight from the freezer on a stick, mango kulfi is both nostalgic and refreshing – a timeless Indian frozen dessert that brings instant relief on warm days and smiles at any gathering.

PREP TIME **15** mins

FREEZING TIME **6** hrs

SERVES **6**

INGREDIENTS

397 ml sweetened condensed milk
240 ml heavy cream
240 ml mango purée
60 ml whole milk
50 g sugar
2 g ground cardamom
10 g pistachios, chopped
10 g almonds, slivered

METHOD

1. In a mixer-grinder, combine the condensed milk, heavy cream, mango purée, whole milk, sugar and cardamom. Blend until smooth and well combined.
2. Pour the mixture into kulfi moulds or small disposable cups.
3. Insert wooden sticks into each mould. If using cups, cover with foil and poke the stick through the centre to hold it upright.
4. Freeze for at least 6 hours or until fully set.
5. To remove from moulds, briefly run warm water over the outside, then gently pull the kulfi out. Garnish with chopped pistachios and almonds, and serve.

AAMRAS

VELVETY MANGO PULP DELIGHT

A celebration of summer, aamras showcases the sweetness and fragrance of Alphonso mangoes. Traditionally served chilled with hot puris, it is a cherished part of Maharashtrian and Gujarati cuisines.

PREP TIME **20** mins
(plus soaking time)

SERVES **4–6**

INGREDIENTS

4 Alphonso mangoes
50 g sugar
2 g green cardamom powder
1 g nutmeg powder
20 g pistachios, slivered
Saffron, a few strands
5 g dried rose petals
Diced mangoes, for garnish

METHOD

1. Soak the mangoes in water for one hour. Remove and peel and chop the mangoes into small pieces.
2. Blend the mango pieces with sugar, cardamom and nutmeg powder in a mixer-grinder until smooth. Adjust the sugar according to the sweetness of the mangoes.
3. If the pulp is too thick, add a little milk or water to reach desired consistency.
4. Transfer to a wide bowl and chill in the refrigerator before serving.
5. To serve, garnish the bowl on the edges with pistachios, saffron and rose petals. Put a few diced mangoes in the centre. Serve with poori, or by itself.

BANANA HALWA

RICH, CARAMELIZED BANANA PUDDING

Deeply aromatic and naturally sweet, banana halwa is a traditional South Indian delicacy that transforms ripe fruit into a rich, glossy confection.

PREP TIME **15** mins COOKING TIME **35–40** mins MAKES **16–20** squares

INGREDIENTS

500 g ripe bananas
250 g jaggery
30 ml water
40 ml ghee (divided)
2 g green cardamom powder
15 g peanuts, roasted
5 g sesame seeds

METHOD

1. Peel the bananas and blend to a smooth paste in a mixer-grinder.
2. In a pan over low heat, dissolve the jaggery in 30 ml water. This will take 4–5 minutes. Bring to a boil and strain to remove impurities if needed. Set aside.
3. In a heavy-bottom pan on medium heat, add 20 g ghee. Once the ghee is hot, add the mashed bananas. Cook on medium heat for 10–12 minutes, stirring continuously, until the mixture thickens and the smell of raw banana disappears.
4. Add the jaggery syrup to the cooked banana mixture. Stir well and continue cooking on low-medium heat, stirring continuously, until all the syrup is mixed well.
5. Add 10 g ghee and continue cooking until all the ghee is absorbed. This will take 3–4 minutes.
6. Add the remaining 10 g ghee. Cook for 5–7 minutes, or until the halwa starts leaving the sides of the pan and turns glossy.
7. Add the cardamom powder and roasted peanuts. Take off the heat.
8. Grease a tray with a little ghee and sprinkle with sesame seeds. Transfer the mixture to the tray, level it evenly and let it cool at room temperature.
9. Once set, invert and cut into squares and serve.

CARROT HALWA

VELVETY, SLOW-COOKED CARROT PUDDING

*

Celebrated for its rich aroma and glowing colour, carrot halwa is served warm in winter or chilled in summer, and is a familiar presence at Indian homes.

PREP TIME **20** mins COOKING TIME **1** hr **35** mins SERVES **8–10**

INGREDIENTS

1 kg carrots
2 L milk
2.5 g citric acid crystals
300 g sugar
120 ml ghee
20 g raisins
20 g dry melon seeds
20 g cashew nuts
12 green cardamoms

METHOD

1. Wash, peel and roughly chop the carrots into 2–3 cm pieces. This makes them easier to cook down and mash evenly later.
2. In a heavy-bottom pan on medium heat, add the carrots and milk. Cook, stirring occasionally, for about 45–50 minutes, or until the milk reduces to about half and the carrots are soft.
3. In a small bowl, dissolve the citric acid crystals with 2 tablespoons water. Add the citric acid solution so that the milk becomes slightly granular in texture.
4. Once the carrots have cooked down, mash them roughly with a potato masher. Continue cooking on medium heat for another 15–20 minutes, stirring often, until most of the remaining milk has thickened and the mixture looks thick and pudding-like, with very little liquid visible at the bottom of the pan. Do not take it off the heat.
5. Add the sugar and mix well. The sugar will draw out moisture and loosen the mixture again. Cook for 10–15 minutes, stirring regularly, until it thickens once more, becomes glossy, and begins to hold its shape when stirred.
6. Now, stir in the ghee. Add the raisins, dry melon seeds and cashews. Cook for 5–10 minutes, stirring continuously, until the halwa starts leaving the sides of the pan.
7. Crush the green cardamom seeds coarsely and add them to the halwa. Mix thoroughly, and take off the heat.
8. Serve warm, garnished with a few extra nuts if desired. It can also be served chilled.

JACKFRUIT HALWA

RICH, STICKY JACKFRUIT FUDGE

The process of extracting starch from dough gives this halwa its distinctive silky texture. Often prepared during jackfruit season, this delicacy reflects the artistry of regional sweet-making traditions.

PREP TIME **3** hrs **30** mins COOKING TIME **45–50** mins MAKES **8–10** pcs

INGREDIENTS

100 g all-purpose flour
820 ml water (divided)
16 ripe jackfruit pods
150 g sugar
1 pinch salt
45 ml ghee
2 g cardamom powder
25 g almonds, slivered

METHOD

1. In a large bowl, combine the flour with 60–70 ml water to form a smooth, medium dough.
2. Place the dough in the centre of the bowl and add 750 ml of water. The dough should be fully covered in water. Rest it for 3 hours.
3. Using your hands, squeeze the dough in the same water, so that the water turns milky. Keep repeating the process till all the starch is washed out from the dough and a small lump is left. This will take 8–10 minutes. Strain the mix and keep the milky water.
4. Add the jackfruit in a mixer-grinder with one cup of milky water and grind to a smooth paste. Now, add 1 cup regular water and blend again. Repeat the process one more time. Pour the batter into the remaining milky water and mix properly.
5. Place a heavy-bottom pan on high flame. Add the jackfruit purée and cook for 12–15 minutes stirring continuously, or until it is thick.
6. Add the sugar and salt. Stir continuously and cook for 8–10 minutes, or until the jackfruit purée is quite thick.

The jackfruit should be ripe and fragrant. This provides natural sweetness, colour and depth of flavour. Cooking the halwa requires constant attention. Continuous stirring prevents sticking and allows uniform reduction. Ghee should be added gradually. This helps the mixture absorb it evenly and develop a glossy finish.

7. Add the ghee in 3 parts, cooking and stirring continuously, till the mixture thickens and leaves the sides of the pan, and becomes a thick mass. This will take 10–12 minutes.
8. Add the cardamom powder and 1/3rd of the chopped almonds. Mix well and cook for another 2–3 minutes until glossy. Take off the heat.
9. Grease a tray with some ghee. Sprinkle the remaining almonds on the greased tray, and pour the mix into the tray while it is still hot.
10. Smoothen the top with a spatula, and let it set slightly.
11. Cool at room temperature for about 2 hours, invert and cut into small cubes with an oiled knife and serve.

TENDER COCONUT PAYASAM

DELICATE, CREAMY COCONUT PUDDING

This payasam blends the subtle sweetness of tender coconut with coconut milk and condensed milk. Served chilled, it is perfect for festive occasions or as a cooling summer treat.

PREP TIME **15** mins

SERVES **5–6**

INGREDIENTS

250 g tender coconut flesh (divided)
150 ml tender coconut water
400 ml coconut milk
400 ml sweetened condensed milk
2 g cardamom powder
40 g chopped mixed nuts, for garnish

METHOD

1. Finely chop 100g of the coconut flesh and set aside. This will be used in the payasam for texture.
2. Take the remaining 150 g coconut flesh and 150 ml tender coconut water in a mixer-grinder and blend into a smooth paste.
3. In a bowl, combine the coconut milk, condensed milk, cardamom powder and the prepared coconut flesh paste. Adjust sweetness according to taste.
4. Add the reserved chopped tender coconut flesh and mix gently.
5. Refrigerate for 1–2 hours. Garnish with the chopped nuts before serving. Best served chilled.

CASHEW NUT BARFI

RICH CASHEW NUT FUDGE

Often known as kaju katli, this barfi is a jewel among Indian sweets. Simple in appearance yet exacting in technique, it is a sweet that rewards precision and patience.

PREP TIME **15** mins COOKING TIME **15–20** mins MAKES **18–20** pcs

INGREDIENTS

150 g cashew nuts

100 g caster sugar

50 ml water

10 ml rose water

10 ml coconut oil

2–3 sheets, edible silver leaf (varq)

METHOD

1. In a mixer-grinder, add the cashew nuts and pulse to a fine powder. Do not over-blend, or the nuts will release oil. Set aside.
2. In a saucepan, combine the caster sugar, water and rose water. Cook on high heat until the syrup reaches 110°C. To check if the syrup has reached the right consistency without a thermometer, add a drop of syrup in cold water. The syrup should form a soft, pliable ball. This will approximately take 3–5 minutes after the sugar has fully dissolved.
3. Add the powdered cashews into the syrup, while stirring continuously.
4. Add the coconut oil and continue cooking for 5–7 minutes, until the mixture thickens and begins to leave the sides of the pan, forming a soft dough.
5. Immediately transfer the mixture onto a parchment paper. Place another parchment sheet on top and roll evenly to 5–10 mm thickness. Remove the top sheet of paper.
6. Place the edible silver leaf on to the mixture. Cut into diamond shapes and allow to rest for 30 minutes before serving.

PISTACHIO & COCONUT SQUARES

NO-BAKE PISTACHIOS & COCONUT TREATS

These elegant confections bring together the richness of pistachios and coconut. Bound with a light sugar-and-glucose syrup, each layer sets into a soft, chewy slab that is both structured and tender.

PREP TIME **15** mins COOKING TIME **10–12** mins MAKES **16–18** pcs

INGREDIENTS

150 ml glucose syrup, (divided)
100 g sugar (divided)
30 ml water (divided)
250 g pistachios
90 g shredded coconut

METHOD

1. To prepare the pistachio layer, in a pot over medium heat, combine 75 ml glucose syrup, 50 g sugar and 15 ml water. Simmer for 2–3 minutes until the sugar dissolves and the mixture slightly thickens.
2. Meanwhile, grease a 8 x 8 inch square dish with a height of about 1.5–2 inches with a little oil or ghee. Set aside.
3. Add the pistachios and stir for 1–2 minutes, or just until evenly coated. Take off the heat and immediately transfer the coated pistachios into the greased tin. Press them flat into an even layer.
4. To prepare the coconut layer, in the same pot over medium heat, cook the remaining 75 ml glucose syrup, 50 g sugar and 15 ml water. Simmer for 2–3 minutes until the sugar dissolves and the mixture slightly thickens.
5. Once the mixture is ready, add the shredded coconut and mix well to coat. Turn off the heat.
6. Transfer the coconut mixture into the tin and spread it evenly over the pistachio layer, pressing it down gently.
7. Allow the layers to cool completely. Once set, remove from the container and with the pistachio side on top, cut into squares.

BHAPA DOI

Silky baked yoghurt

LITCHI FALOODA

Layered litchi rose milk indulgence

MATKA KULFI

Slow-set, creamy earthen pot ice cream

PISTA KULFI

Rich, pistachio-infused ice cream

STRAWBERRY ROSE SHRIKHAND

Creamy strawberry rose yoghurt

FROZEN & CHILLED DESSERTS

BHAPA DOI

SILKY BAKED YOGHURT

Soft and delicate, bhapa doi is a classic Bengali steamed dessert. This baked version recreates the same slow cooking process, resulting in a smooth, melt-in-the-mouth finish.

PREP TIME **15** mins
(plus chilling time)

COOKING TIME **25** mins

SERVES **6–8**

INGREDIENTS

175 g Greek yoghurt
175 g single cream
200 ml condensed milk
5 ml rose essence
Fresh fruits, to serve
Mint leaves, to garnish

METHOD

1. Preheat the oven to 100°C.
2. Grease a loaf pan lightly with ghee. Line the pan with parchment paper on the bottom and sides.
3. In a mixing bowl, whisk together the yoghurt, cream, condensed milk and rose essence until smooth and lump-free.
4. Pour in the mixture into the pan. Cover tightly with aluminium foil.
5. Place the loaf pan inside a larger baking tray. Pour hot water into the larger tray until it reaches halfway up the sides of the loaf pan.
6. Transfer to the oven and bake for 25 minutes. Remove the foil. The mixture should be set around the edges but still a little wobbly in the centre, it will firm up as it cools.
7. Remove from the oven and let it cool to room temperature. Cover with cling film and refrigerate for 4–6 hours, or until fully set.
8. Slice neatly from the loaf pan and garnish with fresh fruits and mint leaves.

LITCHI FALOODA

LAYERED LITCHI ROSE MILK INDULGENCE

Layers of silky chilled milk, tender falooda vermicelli, basil seeds, jelly and juicy litchis come together with rose syrup and vanilla ice cream to create a dessert that is as beautiful as it is indulgent.

PREP TIME **20** min (plus chilling time)

COOKING TIME **10** mins

SERVES **4**

INGREDIENTS

20 g basil seeds

5 g cornflour

500 ml full-fat milk

25 g sugar

620 ml water (divided)

50 g falooda vermicelli (sev), dried

1 packet raspberry / strawberry jelly

90 ml rose syrup

200 g fresh or canned litchis, deseeded

200 g vanilla ice cream

20 g chopped nuts

Candied cherry, for garnish

METHOD

1. Soak the basil seeds in 120 ml water for 30 minutes.
2. Meanwhile, in a small bowl, dissolve the cornflour in 2 tablespoons of milk. Set aside.
3. Pour the milk in a pot and place over low heat and bring to a boil. Once it starts boiling, add the cornflour mix and sugar. Allow it to come to a boil again, then remove from heat.
4. Allow to cool for 7–10 minutes. Cover with cling film, pressing it directly onto the surface to prevent a skin from forming. Cool to room temperature, then refrigerate until well chilled.
5. In another vessel over medium heat, bring the remaining 500 ml water to a boil and add the falooda sev. Cook the falooda sev for 5–6 minutes, or until soft. Drain and rinse under cold water.
6. Make jelly as per the directions on the packet and once set, cut into cubes.
7. To assemble the falooda, take a tall glass, add a few tablespoons of rose syrup, then add in the falooda sev, chopped litchi, soaked basil seeds and jelly cubes. Pour in about 120–150 ml chilled thickened milk. Top with 1 scoop vanilla ice cream.
8. Garnish with nuts and a drizzle of rose syrup. Top with a candied cherry. Serve immediately with a long spoon and straw.

MATKA KULFI

SLOW-SET, CREAMY EARTHEN POT ICE CREAM

Slow-simmered milk, spices and a generous blend of nuts come together in this frozen treat. The porous matkas subtly enhance the flavour while keeping the kulfi beautifully chilled.

PREP TIME **30** mins (plus soaking & freezing time)

FREEZING TIME **6–8** hrs

SERVES **6–8**

INGREDIENTS

6 / 8 earthenware pots (matka)
25 g almonds, soaked overnight

20 g cashew nuts

2 g green cardamom powder

Saffron, a few strands
+ a few strands for garnish

4 black peppercorns

1.5 L full-fat milk (divided)

150 g sugar (divided)

METHOD

1. Soak the matkas (earthenware pots) in water for a minimum of 2–3 hours.
2. Peel the almonds and transfer to a mixer-grinder with the cashew nuts, cardamom powder, saffron and peppercorns. Grind to a powder, then add 100 ml milk and make a smooth paste.
3. Pour the remaining milk into a heavy-bottom pan. Bring to a boil on medium heat, then reduce heat to low and simmer, stirring occasionally to prevent sticking. Let it reduce to about half of the original volume. This will take 30–40 minutes.
4. In another heavy-bottom pan, add 50 g sugar and cook on low heat for 5–7 minutes. Do not stir until the sugar melts and turns a light amber colour. Swirl the pan gently for even caramelization.
5. Add the caramelized sugar to the reduced milk along with the remaining 100 g sugar.
6. Add the prepared nut paste and stir well. Continue cooking the milk for another 15–20 minutes, or until it is reduced to about 1/3rd of the original quantity. Remove from heat and let the mixture cool to room temperature.
7. Fill the matkas with the kulfi mix, cover with foil and freeze for at least 6–8 hours, or overnight. To serve, garnish the kulfi with a few strands of saffron and chopped nuts.

PISTA KULFI

RICH, PISTACHIO-INFUSED ICE CREAM

Rich, dense and intensely fragrant, this kulfi is a celebration of slow cooking and flavours. Finished with a sprinkle of slivered pistachios, it is perfect for hot days and festive feasts alike.

PREP TIME **20** mins (plus freezing time)

COOKING TIME **45–50** mins

MAKES **6–8** kulfis

INGREDIENTS

1.1 L full-fat milk (divided)

60 g pistachios

+ 20 g pistachios, slivered, for garnish

100 g sugar

2 g green cardamom powder

Saffron, a few strands

30 g milk powder

METHOD

1. Pour 1 L milk into a heavy-bottom pan over medium heat and bring to a boil. Reduce heat and simmer on low, stirring frequently, for 6–8 minutes or until the milk reduces to half its original volume.
2. Meanwhile, grind the pistachios, sugar, cardamom powder and saffron together to a fine powder. Place in a bowl and add the milk powder. Add the remaining 100 ml milk and combine well to a smooth paste.
3. Add this paste to the reduced milk. Allow it to cook for 10–12 minutes, or until quite thick.
4. Remove from heat and let the mixture cool to room temperature. Pour the prepared mixture into kulfi moulds or small cups. Cover and freeze for at least 6–8 hours, or overnight.
5. To demould the kulfi, run the moulds under warm water for a few seconds. Remove to a serving platter, garnish with slivered pistachios and serve.

STRAWBERRY ROSE SHRIKHAND

CREAMY STRAWBERRY ROSE YOGHURT

Light, creamy and delicately fragrant, this strawberry rose shrikhand is a refreshing twist on the classic Indian yoghurt dessert.

PREP TIME **20** mins
(plus time for draining the yoghurt)

COOKING TIME **5–7** mins

SERVES **6–8**

INGREDIENTS

750 g full-fat yoghurt

250 g strawberries

+100 g strawberry slices, for garnish

50 g sugar

50 g icing sugar

5 ml rose water

50 g whipping cream

Fresh / dried rose petals, for garnish

METHOD

1. Line a sieve or strainer with a muslin cloth or cheesecloth. Place the yoghurt in it and let it drain for a minimum of 2–3 hours or leave overnight in the fridge to remove excess whey.
2. Place a heavy-bottom pot on medium-low heat and add 200 g strawberries, along with the sugar. Cook the strawberries for 6–8 minutes or until they are soft. Remove from heat.
3. Allow the strawberries to cool. Transfer them to a mixer-grinder and blend into a smooth purée. Set aside.
4. Transfer the hung yoghurt to a mixing bowl. Add the icing sugar and rose water. Whisk until smooth and creamy. Add the cream and whisk again.
5. Chop the remaining strawberries and add to the yoghurt mix. Gently fold in strawberry purée until fully incorporated.
6. Cover and refrigerate for at least 1–2 hours for the flavours to meld. Spoon into serving bowls. Garnish with the fresh strawberry slices and rose petals.

DATE & CASHEW NUT FUDGE
Rich fudge with dates & cashew nuts

BADAM HALWA
Almond pudding with ghee & saffron

CHIA KHEER
No-cook chia seed & jaggery pudding

FENNEL SEED PANCAKES WITH PLUM COMPOTE
Spiced pancakes served with fruit compote

FLAXSEED LADOO
Flaxseed balls with nuts & coconut

MAKHANA KHEER
A classical Indian dessert made with fox nuts

NANKHATAI
Indian shortbread

NOLEN GUR SANDESH
Curd cheese & date plum jaggery fudge

OATS & JAGGERY KHEER
Oats & jaggery pudding

RAGI LADOO
Sweet finger millet flour balls

HEALTHY TWISTS

DATE & CASHEW NUT FUDGE

RICH FUDGE WITH DATES & CASHEW NUTS

*

Sweet dates form the base, while milk, butter and condensed milk lend a soft, melt-in-the-mouth texture. It is perfect for festive gifting, afternoon tea, or whenever you crave a wholesome sweet.

PREP TIME **15** mins
(plus soaking time)

COOKING TIME **20–25** mins

MAKES **20–22** pcs

INGREDIENTS

350 g dates, pitted

500 ml milk

60 g unsalted butter, melted (divided)

50 g sugar

55 ml condensed milk

50 g cashew nuts, chopped

40 g dried melon seeds

40 g golden raisins

3 g green cardamom powder

METHOD

1. In a medium-size bowl, soak the dates in milk for 2–3 hours, or until the dates turn soft.
2. Transfer the soaked dates and milk to a mixer-grinder. Blitz into a smooth, thick paste.
3. Place a heavy-bottom pan over low heat and pour in the prepared date purée. Stirring continuously, cook for 5 minutes or until thick.
4. Stir in 30 g melted butter and cook for 5 minutes, making sure that the butter is fully incorporated.
5. Add the sugar, condensed milk, cashew nuts, melon seeds, raisins and cardamom powder. Stir well to mix and cook gently, ensuring it doesn't stick.
6. Now, add in the remaining 30 g butter. Cook for 8–10 minutes stirring continuously until the mixture comes together as a thick, sticky fudge.
7. Transfer to a greased tray. Spread the mixture to about 1.5 cm thickness. Allow to cool to room temperature, then cut into 5 cm squares (or diagonally into triangles). This is perfect with a cup of tea or coffee.

BADAM HALWA

ALMOND PUDDING WITH, GHEE & SAFFRON

*

Often reserved for special occasions, badam halwa is served in small portions, to be savoured slowly.

PREP TIME **45** mins COOKING TIME **35–40** mins SERVES **8–10**

INGREDIENTS

500 g almonds
300 g sugar
400 g water
1 pinch saffron
+ a few strands, for garnish
300 g ghee
40 g wheat flour
Slivered pistachios, for garnish
Slivered almonds, for garnish

METHOD

1. Place the almonds in a pot over medium heat, with enough water to cover them completely. Boil for about 10–12 minutes, or until the skin peels off easily. Turn off the heat.
2. Pour the boiled almonds into a strainer and peel them while they are hot. Rub with a cloth and dry the almonds.
3. In a mixer-grinder, add the peeled almonds in batches and grind them. Make sure you grind them granular.
4. To make the syrup, place the sugar and water in a pot on medium heat. Once it comes to a boil, lower the heat and add the saffron. Let it infuse for a few minutes. Keep the syrup warm on very low heat while preparing the halwa.
5. Heat the ghee in a heavy-bottom pan. Once the ghee is hot, add the wheat flour and roast for 4–5 minutes on low-medium heat until it turns golden and aromatic. Stir continuously to prevent burning.
6. Add the ground almonds to the roasted wheat flour. Mix well and cook for 4–5 minutes, stirring continuously, until the mixture turns golden.
7. Slowly pour the warm sugar syrup into the halwa mixture, stirring continuously to avoid lumps.
8. Reduce the heat to low and cook, stirring often, for 10–15 minutes until the halwa starts to leave the sides of the pan and reaches a thick cohesive consistency. Transfer the halwa to a serving dish.
9. Garnish with slivered pistachios, almonds and a few saffron strands. Serve warm.

CHIA KHEER

A NO-COOK CHIA SEED & JAGGERY PUDDING

*

This healthy take on kheer, blends traditional flavours with nourishing ingredients. Finished with seasonal fruits and nuts, it makes for a refreshing breakfast, a mindful dessert, or a wholesome snack.

PREP TIME **10** mins | SOAKING TIME **6–8** hrs | SERVES **2–3**

INGREDIENTS

30 g chia seeds

250 ml almond milk

100 ml coconut milk (optional, else replace with an additional **100ml** almond milk)

30 g grated jaggery

2 g green cardamom powder

1 tbsp sliced almonds

6 strawberries, halved

50 g blueberries

METHOD

1. In a bowl or jar, combine the chia seeds, almond milk, coconut milk (if using), grated jaggery and cardamom powder. Stir well.
2. Cover and refrigerate overnight (or at least 6–8 hours). The chia seeds will absorb the liquid and thicken into a pudding-like consistency.
3. In the morning, stir the kheer. If it is too thick, add a splash of almond milk to loosen it.
4. Garnish with sliced almonds, strawberries and blueberries. The kheer can stay in the fridge for 2–3 days.

FENNEL SEED PANCAKES WITH PLUM COMPOTE

SPICED PANCAKES SERVED WITH A FRUIT COMPOTE

These pancakes, paired with a tart compote are perfect for weekend breakfasts or relaxed brunches.

PREP TIME **30** min COOKING TIME **25–30** min SERVES **4**

INGREDIENTS

For the Orange Honey

100 g honey
Zest of 1 orange

For the Pancakes

2 green cardamom pods
2 tsp fennel seeds
300 g all-purpose flour
60 g fine semolina
180 g caster sugar
1 tsp baking powder
1 pinch salt
375 ml milk
Ghee, for frying

For the Plum Compote

500 g plums
100 g sugar
60 ml water
15 ml lemon juice
1-inch cinnamon stick
1 star anise

To Serve

Flaked almonds, toasted
Cream, whipped softly

METHOD

1. To prepare orange honey, mix the zest of orange and honey in a bottle and preferably, leave overnight.
2. For the pancakes, place the cardamom seeds and fennel in a mortar and pestle and pound to a coarse powder – they should be aromatic but not too fine.
3. In a mixing bowl, whisk the ground spices with flour, semolina, sugar, baking powder, a pinch of salt and milk into a thick batter. Let it rest for 10 minutes.
4. To prepare the plum compote, wash, halve and pit the plums. Cut the plums into quarters if they are large.
5. In a saucepan over low–medium heat, add the prepped plums, sugar, water and lemon juice. Add the cinnamon and star anise.
6. Heat gently until the sugar dissolves, then simmer over low–medium heat for 10–12 minutes until the plums soften and release juices. Mash lightly with the back of a spoon. Remove the spices. Take it off the heat and let cool to room temperature.
7. Heat a little ghee in a frying pan over medium–low heat. Add about 1/4th cup of batter per pancake. Cook for 3–4 minutes until golden underneath. Flip, then reduce heat and cook gently for 5–6 minutes until cooked through. Repeat with the remaining batter.
8. To serve, place the pancakes on a platter, drizzle with orange honey and sprinkle with toasted almond flakes. Add whipped cream on top and serve with the plum compote on the side.

FLAXSEED LADOO

FLAXSEED BALLS WITH NUTS & COCONUT

*

These nutritious, wholesome ladoos are a nourishing take on the traditional Indian ladoo.

PREP TIME **20** mins COOKING TIME **25** mins MAKES **15–18** pcs

INGREDIENTS

250 g flaxseeds, unsalted
60 ml ghee (divided)
30 g almonds
30 g walnuts
15 g fox nuts (makhana)
20 g desiccated coconut
200 g jaggery, grated
20 g raisins
2 g cardamom powder
1 g nutmeg powder

METHOD

1. In a pan over low heat, dry roast the flaxseeds until they start popping and release a nutty aroma. Let it cool, then add the flaxseeds to a mixer-grinder and grind to a coarse powder. Do not grind the flaxseeds too fine as it turns oily.
2. In another pan over medium heat, heat 10 ml ghee, add the almonds and roast for 3–4 minutes. Remove the almonds and set aside. In the same pan, add walnuts and roast for 2–3 minutes. Remove and set aside.
3. In the same pan, roast the makhanas for 3–4 minutes till light brown. Remove and set aside. Add the desiccated coconut and roast for 1–2 minutes, or until it starts to change colour. Set aside to cool.
4. Add the roasted almonds, walnuts and makhanas to a mixer-grinder and grind to a coarse powder. Mix with the roasted desiccated coconut.
5. Heat 40 g ghee in a heavy-bottom pan. Add the jaggery and heat on low flame for 2–3 minutes, or until it melts, stirring continuously. Don't cook after the jaggery is melted, otherwise the ladoos will become hard.
6. Mix the ground flaxseeds, the crushed nuts-makhana powder, raisins, cardamom and nutmeg powder in a large, wide pan. Pour the hot jaggery and combine using a spatula. Mix well so everything is coated.
7. Add the remaining ghee, and mix thoroughly. Grease your palms and while the mixture is warm, roll into ladoos. Let them cool fully before storing in an airtight container.

MAKHANA KHEER

A CLASSICAL INDIAN DESSERT MADE WITH FOX NUTS

This makhana-based kheer offers a wholesome twist on the traditional Indian kheer.

PREP TIME **15** mins | COOKING TIME **20** mins | SERVES **4**

INGREDIENTS

40 g ghee (divided)
250 g fox nuts (makhana)
50 g almonds
50 g cashew nuts
100 g milk powder
3 g green cardamom powder
Saffron, a few strands
1 L milk
50 g sugar (or stevia or agave syrup)

METHOD

1. Heat 30 ghee in a pan on medium heat. Add the makhana and roast gently until they turn crisp. This usually takes 8–10 minutes. Keep stirring to avoid burning. Remove from heat and let it cool slightly.
2. Add the remaining ghee and add the almonds and roast for 3–4 minutes, until light brown. Remove from heat and set aside.
3. Add the cashew nuts in the ghee and roast for 2–3 minutes, or until golden. Remove from heat and set aside.
4. Reserve about 1/2 cup of the roasted makhana and nuts. Crush them coarsely using a mortar and pestle or a rolling pin. Put the rest of makhanas and nuts in a blender and grind to a fine powder.
5. In a bowl, combine the finely- and coarsely-ground roasted makhana-nut mix, milk powder, cardamom powder and saffron. Mix well. The premix is ready.
6. In a heavy-bottom pan over medium heat, bring the milk to a gentle boil. Reduce the heat and simmer for 5–7 minutes.
7. Add 6–7 tbsp of the prepared premix to the milk, stirring continuously to prevent lumps. Cook for 10–12 minutes on low heat until the kheer thickens slightly.
8. Add the sugar, or stevia or agave syrup. If using stevia, start small, it is potent, so adjust according to taste. Mix well and take off the heat. Serve warm or chilled, garnished with a few extra chopped nuts or a pinch of saffron, if desired.

NANKHATAI

INDIAN SHORTBREAD

A beloved treat with roots in colonial-era bakeries and Irani cafés. Made with a blend of flour, besan and semolina, these cookies strike a beautiful balance between richness and lightness.

PREP TIME **15** mins COOKING TIME **18–20** mins MAKES **16–18** pcs

INGREDIENTS

100 g soft unsalted butter
100 g caster sugar
60 g all-purpose flour
60 g gram flour (besan)
60 g semolina
3 g baking soda
20 g sunflower seeds

METHOD

1. In a mixing bowl, cream the butter and sugar together for about 3 minutes until light, smooth and creamy.
2. Sift and combine the all-purpose flour, besan, semolina and baking soda. Add this dry mix into the butter–sugar mixture. Mix until it comes together into a soft dough.
3. Divide the dough into 25 g portions and roll into smooth balls.
4. Preheat the oven to 190°C.
5. Place the dough balls on a lined baking sheet, slightly flatten each with your fingers, and sprinkle sunflower seeds on top.
6. Bake for 18–20 minutes, or until golden brown. Cool on a wire rack before serving.

NOLEN GUR SANDESH

CURD CHEESE & DATE PALM JAGGERY FUDGE

Soft, fragrant and delicately sweet, nolen gur sandesh is one of Bengal's most cherished winter confections. The fleeting season of nolen gur makes this dessert especially precious.

PREP TIME **1** hr | COOKING TIME **10–15** mins | MAKES **12–15** pcs

INGREDIENTS

2 L cow's milk

2 pinches alum (or 2 tbsp white vinegar)

100 ml water

15 g corn starch

60 ml liquid or soft palm date jaggery (nolen gur)

1 pinch green cardamom powder

Saffron, a few strands

METHOD

1. Place the cow's milk in a heavy-bottom pan and bring to a boil on high heat. Once it comes to a boil, lower the heat.
2. In a small bowl dissolve the alum in 100 ml water. Add 1–2 tsp alum mixture gradually to the milk while stirring. The milk will curdle and the whey will separate.
3. Strain the curdled milk through a muslin cloth to collect the chenna. Wash the chenna under cold running water to remove the taste of alum. Knot the muslin cloth and hang the cloth for 30–40 minutes to drain excess water.
4. Transfer the drained chenna to a plate. Knead it with the heel of your palm for 8–10 minutes until smooth and soft. Add corn starch and continue kneading till it is well incorporated.
5. Heat a nonstick pan on low flame. Add the kneaded paneer, nolen gur and cardamom powder. Mix well and cook for 2–3 minutes until the mixture thickens and leaves the sides of the pan. Do not overcook, or the sandesh will turn crumbly.
6. Remove from heat and transfer to a flat plate. Spread and let it cool slightly. While still warm, divide into small portions and shape into flat rounds or use traditional wooden sandesh moulds to shape them.
7. Dissolve the saffron in 30 ml water. Brush lightly with dissolved saffron or place a drop in the centre. Allow to set for 30 minutes. Serve fresh.

OATS & JAGGERY KHEER

OATS & JAGGERY PUDDING

Finished with toasted nuts, raisins and fresh pomegranate seeds, this kheer is suitable for both festive offerings and everyday indulgence. It is a reminder that dessert can be both satisfying and healthy.

PREP TIME **10** mins   COOKING TIME **15** mins   SERVES **2–3**

INGREDIENTS

125 ml water
75 g jaggery
10 ml ghee
25 g cashew nuts
10 g raisins
50 g rolled oats
500 ml coconut milk
1 g cardamom powder
20 g pomegranate arils

METHOD

1. In a small saucepan, add the water and jaggery. Cook over low heat, until the jaggery melts completely. Strain to remove impurities and set aside.
2. Heat the ghee in a pan over low heat. Add the cashew nuts and roast for 2–3 minutes, or until golden brown. Remove and set aside.
3. Add the raisins and fry for 1–2 minutes, or until they puff up. Remove and set aside.
4. Lightly roast the oats in the same pan for 1–2 minutes.
5. Pour in the coconut milk and simmer for 5–6 minutes on medium heat. Stir occasionally until the oats turn soft and the mixture thickens. Add a little water, if required.
6. Slowly add the jaggery syrup to the oats-coconut milk mixture, stirring continuously. Simmer gently for 2–3 minutes. Avoid boiling vigorously to prevent coconut milk from splitting.
7. Stir in the cardamom powder. Garnish with the roasted cashews, raisins and a few pomegranate arils. Serve warm or chilled.

RAGI LADOO

SWEET FINGER MILLET FLOUR BALLS

A healthy twist on traditional Indian sweets, these energy-packed ladoos are perfect as a nutritious snack, post-workout treat, or nourishing dessert for all ages.

PREP TIME **15** mins COOKING TIME **15–20** mins MAKES **15–18** pcs

INGREDIENTS

30 ml ghee
120 g finger millet (ragi) flour
30 g walnuts, chopped
20 g desiccated coconut
150 g jaggery
60 ml water
4 g dry ginger powder
0.5 g nutmeg powder

METHOD

1. Heat the ghee in a heavy-bottom pan. Add the ragi flour and roast on low flame for 8–10 minutes, until it gives a nutty aroma and changes colour slightly. Keep stirring to avoid burning. Remove from heat and let it cool.
2. In a heavy-bottom pan on low heat, add the walnuts and dry roast for just 2–3 minutes. Ensure that they don't change colour. Remove from heat and set aside.
3. In the same pan, add the desiccated coconut and dry roast for just 2–3 minutes, without changing colour. Remove from heat and set aside.
4. In another pan over low heat, add the jaggery and water. Heat on low until the jaggery melts completely. Strain to remove impurities, then return to the pan. Boil until it reaches a soft ball consistency (drop a little syrup in cold water, it should form a soft ball), and turn off the heat. Set aside.
5. Now add the roasted coconut, walnuts, dry ginger powder and nutmeg in the pan with the roasted ragi. Mix well. Pour the hot jaggery syrup gradually into the flour mixture. Mix quickly with a spoon (it will be hot) until everything is well combined.
6. Grease your palms with a little ghee and shape the dough into small ladoos while warm. Allow the ladoos to cool completely. Store in an airtight container for up to 7–10 days.

APPENDICES

CONVERSION CHART

INGREDIENT	STANDARD	METRIC	IMPERIAL
Ghee	1 cup	213 g	7.5 oz
Oil	1 cup	236 ml / 217 g	7.5 oz
Milk	1 cup	236 ml	8 oz
Yoghurt	1 cup	244 g	8.5 oz
Butter	1 cup	240 g	8 oz
Cream	1 cup	227 g	8.5 oz
Coconut Milk	1 cup	232 g	8 oz
Caster Sugar	1 cup / 1 tbsp	118 g / 7 g	5 oz
Granulated Sugar	1 cup	201 g	7 oz
Jaggery	1 cup	213 g	7.5 oz
Gram flour	1 cup	113 g	4 oz
All-purpose flour	1 cup	125 g	4 oz
Finger millet flour	1 cup	127 g	4.5 oz
Cornflour	1 cup	130 g	4.5 oz
Whole wheat flour	1 cup	118 g	4 oz

INGREDIENT	STANDARD	METRIC	IMPERIAL
Semolina	1 cup	163 g	5.5 oz
Coconut (grated)	1 cup	80 g	2.82 oz
Coconut (desiccated)	1 cup	60 g	2.12 oz
Baking Soda / Baking powder	1 tbsp	13 g	0.5 oz
All powdered spices	1 tbsp	10 g	0.35 oz
Fennel seeds	1 tbsp	7.5 g	0.26 oz
Almonds (peeled)	1 cup	140 g	4.94 oz
Almonds (slivered)	1 cup	128 g	4.52 oz
Almonds (chopped)	1 cup	130 g	4.59 oz
Pistachio (shelled)	1 cup	123 g	4.34 oz
Pistachio (slivered)	1 cup	100 g	3.53 oz
Pistachio (chopped)	1 cup	100 g	3.53 oz
Raisins	1 cup	45 g	1.59 oz
Walnuts	1 cup	120 g	4.23 oz
Cashew nuts (chopped)	1 cup	128 g	4.52 oz

SUBSTITUTIONS

Many mithai recipes can be adapted with simple substitutions, that are available locally. These changes may slightly alter the flavour or texture, but they will produce delicious results.

Ghee

Ghee is often essential for its rich flavour, but unsalted butter can be used in its place. Butter has a slightly higher water content, so recipes may be a little softer.

Spice

Cardamom may be replaced with cinnamon or nutmeg for a different but equally warming flavour profile.

Jaggery

Jaggery may be substituted with brown sugar when unavailable, though the flavour will be milder and less caramel-like

Boora Sugar

Caster sugar can be used instead of boora sugar in recipes that call for a finer texture.

Coconut

Fresh coconut can often be replaced with desiccated coconut, provided it is lightly soaked first to restore some moisture

Nuts

For nut allergies, almonds, pistachios and cashew nuts can often be replaced with seeds such as pumpkin or sunflower seeds.

Rose Water

Rose water and kewra water can be used interchangeably in many recipes, depending on personal preference.

Milk

In milk-based desserts, evaporated milk can often be used to shorten cooking time, while plant-based milks may work in some recipes, though they may produce a slightly different texture and taste.

Khoya / Mawa

Khoya or mawa can be difficult to find outside India; in many recipes it can be replaced with milk powder combined with cream or condensed milk to create a similar richness.

STORAGE

Indian mithai keeps best when stored carefully, as factors such as moisture, milk content and climate can affect both texture and shelf life.

1. Airtight containers are essential to prevent mithai from drying out or absorbing odours from other foods
2. Sweets should always be cooled completely before storing, as any trapped steam can create condensation and lead to spoilage.
3. In warmer climates, refrigeration may help extend the freshness of mithai. Refrigerated sweets should however be brought back to room temperature before serving, as this restores both their flavour and texture
4. Dry sweets such as ladoos and barfi made without fresh dairy and roasted nut-based mithai can usually be kept at room temperature for 5–7 days in a cool, dry place.
5. Milk-based and chenna sweets such as rasgulla, rasmalai, kalakand, peda and kheer are more delicate and should always be stored in the refrigerator. Most are best consumed within 2–3 days.
6. Syrup-soaked sweets can often last up to 4–5 days if kept chilled in a covered container.
7. Fried sweets such as gulab jamun can be refrigerated for several days, though they should be reheated gently before serving.
8. For longer storage, many mithai can be frozen successfully. Wrap portions tightly and freeze for up to one month. Thaw overnight in the refrigerator and bring to room temperature before serving.
9. In general, always check for changes in smell, texture or colour before eating, and when in doubt, discard any mithai that no longer appears fresh.

GLOSSARY

Atta: Wholemeal wheat flour with a slightly nutty flavour, traditionally used in halwa and warming winter sweets.

Badam: The Hindi word for almonds, a staple ingredient in Indian confectionery.

Barfi / Burfi: A dense, fudge-like sweet made from milk solids, sugar and flavourings such as nuts, spices or fruit.

Basmati Rice: Fragrant long-grain rice used in creamy milk desserts such as kheer and phirni.

Besan / Gram Flour: Flour ground from split chickpeas, widely used in ladoos, burfi and halwa.

Boiling Point: The stage at which a sugar syrup or milk base reaches a vigorous, rolling simmer.

Boora Sugar: Fine, unrefined sugar with a soft, slightly crumbly texture, favoured in traditional Indian sweets.

Cardamom / Elaichi: A fragrant spice prized for its warm, floral notes; one of the most widely used aromatics in mithai.

Cashew Nut: A rich, creamy nut used as both a key ingredient and a garnish in sweets such as kaju katli.

Chana Dal: Split Bengal gram used as a base in some halwas and sweet fillings.

Chashni: Sugar syrup cooked to specific consistencies, essential for sweets such as gulab jamun, jalebi and imarti.

Chenna: Fresh curd cheese made by curdling warm milk with lemon juice or vinegar; the foundation of rasgulla and sandesh.

Chikki: A crisp, brittle sweet made by cooking jaggery or sugar with nuts or seeds until set.

Clove: An intensely aromatic spice occasionally added to festive sweets and spiced syrups.

Coarse Sugar: Large sugar crystals used to add texture, sparkle, or a decorative finish to sweets.

Coconut: Fresh or dried coconut used throughout Indian confectionery in ladoos, barfi and stuffed sweet fillings.

Condensed Milk: Sweetened milk reduced to a thick, pourable consistency; often used to simplify and speed up mithai recipes.

Cornflour: A fine starch used occasionally to thicken milk mixtures or sweet fillings.

Date: Naturally sweet, caramel-rich fruit often blended into healthier or no-cook mithai.

Deep Frying: A cooking method used for sweets such as gulab jamun, jalebi and gujiya, producing a golden, crisp exterior.

Dry Fruits: A collective term for nuts and dried fruits – including almonds, cashews, pistachios and raisins – widely used across Indian sweets.

Fennel Seed: Small, aromatic seeds that lend a gently sweet, anise-like flavour to sweets and mouth fresheners.

Garnish: Decorative finishing touches – such as slivered nuts, edible petals, or silver leaf – applied to completed sweets.

Ghee: Clarified butter with a rich, nutty aroma; an essential fat in the making of many traditional Indian sweets.

Gond: Edible gum crystals that puff up when fried in ghee, adding a light, crunchy texture to winter sweets and ladoos.

Gujiya: A crescent-shaped fried pastry filled with a mixture of khoya, coconut and nuts, especially popular at Holi.

Halwa: A broad family of soft, rich sweets made from ingredients such as semolina, lentils, flour, or vegetables, cooked slowly in ghee.

Honey: A natural sweetener with floral complexity, sometimes used in place of refined sugar in contemporary mithai.

Imarti: A flower-shaped batter sweet, deep-fried and soaked in fragrant sugar syrup; similar in concept to jalebi.

Jaggery: Unrefined cane or palm sugar with a deep, earthy caramel flavour, used extensively in traditional Indian sweets.

Jaggery Syrup: Jaggery melted and cooked with water until smooth, used as a natural sweetening syrup.

Jalebi: Crisp, golden spirals of fermented batter, deep-fried and soaked in sugar syrup until glossy and sweet.

Kaju Katli: Thin, diamond-shaped sweets made from finely ground cashews and sugar, often finished with silver leaf.

Kesar: The Hindi word for saffron.

Kesari: A saffron-scented semolina sweet, vibrant in colour and delicately spiced.

Khoya / Mawa: Milk solids reduced by slow cooking until thick and rich; the base for barfi, peda and gujiya fillings.

Ladoo: Round, palm-sized sweets made from flour, nuts, seeds, or coconut, bound together with ghee and sugar.

Lotus Seeds / Makhana: Light, crisp fox nuts used in fasting-friendly sweets and creamy puddings.

Malai: The thick, velvety cream that collects on the surface of slowly boiled full-fat milk.

Milk Powder: Dried skimmed or whole milk used as a convenient shortcut in quick-cook peda and gulab jamun recipes.

Modak: Steamed or fried sweet dumplings filled with coconut and jaggery, traditionally prepared for Ganesh Chaturthi.

Nutmeg: A warm, subtly sweet spice used in small quantities to add depth to festive mithai.

Paneer: Fresh Indian cheese with a mild, milky flavour, sometimes used in place of chenna in certain sweets.

Peanuts: Affordable and widely used in chikki, brittle and some ladoo recipes.

Peda: Small, soft milk-based sweets, often flavoured with cardamom or saffron and moulded into decorative rounds.

Phirni: A silky, chilled dessert made from coarsely ground rice simmered in sweetened, flavoured milk.

Pistachio: A vibrant green nut widely used as a garnish and flavouring, adding both colour and a pleasant crunch to mithai.

Poppy Seed: Tiny, mildly nutty seeds used in sweet fillings, as a garnish and in some regional sweets.

Rabri: Sweetened full-fat milk simmered for an extended time until thick, creamy and layered with clotted cream.

Rasgulla: Soft, spongy cheese dumplings made from chenna and cooked in light sugar syrup.

Rasmalai: Flattened chenna patties served chilled in thickened, saffron-scented milk.

Rava: Another name for semolina, used interchangeably with sooji across regional recipes.

Rice Flour: Finely milled rice used in steamed sweets, batters and some regional mithai.

Roasted Semolina: Semolina toasted in ghee until golden and fragrant, essential to halwa, sheera and kesari.

Roasting: The technique of cooking an ingredient – such as semolina, nuts, or flour – in ghee or over dry heat to develop a deeper, nuttier flavour.

Rose / Gulab Water: Distilled floral essence that adds a delicate rose fragrance to a wide range of Indian sweets.

Sabudana: Small tapioca pearls that become translucent and chewy when cooked, often used in fasting-day desserts.

Saffron: The world's most prized spice, used in the smallest quantities to impart a warm golden colour and honeyed aroma.

Sandesh: A refined Bengali sweet made from fresh chenna and shaped by hand or mould.

Semolina: Coarsely or finely milled wheat used across numerous sweets, including halwa, sheera and ladoos.

Sheera: A semolina-based sweet similar to halwa, often made quickly with ghee, sugar and warm milk.

Shrikhand: A creamy, chilled dessert made from strained yoghurt, sweetened and flavoured with saffron, cardamom, or fresh fruit.

Silver Leaf / Varq: Delicate edible foil made from pure silver, used to decorate premium mithai with an elegant, lustrous finish.

Simmering: Gentle, sustained cooking over low heat, particularly important when reducing milk-based sweets to prevent scorching.

Skimming: The technique of removing cream, foam, or impurities from the surface of simmering milk or sugar syrup.

Slivered Nuts: Thin, elegant slices of almonds or pistachios used to finish and garnish Indian sweets.

Sooji: Fine semolina used in halwa, kesari, and other sweets; used interchangeably with rava in many recipes.

Sugar Syrup: A cooked solution of sugar and water brought to a specific consistency to soak, glaze or bind sweets.

Tempering: The technique of briefly heating spices, nuts, or other aromatics in ghee before incorporating them to release maximum flavour.

Toasting: Lightly cooking nuts, seeds, or coconut in a dry pan to intensify their flavour and add crunch.

Unsalted Butter: Butter without added salt, used as a substitute when ghee is unavailable.

Vermicelli: Fine wheat noodles used in seviyan kheer, a fragrant, milk-based pudding popular at festivals and celebrations.

Whisking: Vigorous beating of ingredients to achieve a smooth, or aerated consistency.

Yoghurt: Fermented milk with a pleasingly tangy flavour, used in shrikhand and as a souring agent in some batters.

Zafran: A Persian-origin word for saffron, widely used in Indian culinary contexts interchangeably with kesar.

ACKNOWLEDGEMENTS

This cookbook was never truly mine to write alone. It arrived the way all good things do – slowly, through the hands and hearts of others.

To my family and friends: you are the first taste of everything. Your patience gave me space to experiment, your love gave me reason to persist, and your honest opinions – offered over sticky fingers and tea-stained afternoons – quietly shaped every page. You turned a kitchen project into something that felt like home.

My deepest gratitude belongs to the home cooks, the sweet makers and the elders who carry generations of knowledge in their hands. Indian mithai is not merely confection; it is memory pressed into form – the saffron of a wedding morning, the cardamom of a grandmother's kitchen, the warmth of celebration passed from one pair of hands to another. To everyone who shared a story, demonstrated a technique, or trusted me with a recipe that had never been written down: this book exists because of you.

To the editors, and designers who transformed a raw manuscript and scattered sugar into something luminous – thank you for seeing what this book could be before it fully was. Your craft gave *Mithai* the visual language it deserves.

And to you, the reader: You are the final, most essential ingredient. Whether you are feeding a festival, honouring a memory, or making Indian sweets for the very first time, may these recipes find their way from your kitchen to your table, and from your table into the hearts of everyone you love.

Arguably, the most universal of Indian sweets, the laddu or ladoo can be found pan-India. States, with their differing cultures, have adapted this mithai to create their own unique versions.

INDEX

Image Credits
Anshika Varma: Pages 2, 29, 37, 127, 155, 160
Pexels: Pages 13 (*above, left & right*), 14 (*below, right*)
iStock: Pages 9 (*above, right; below, left & right*), 13 (*below, left*), 14 (*below, left*)
All images not otherwise credited are from the author.

Published in India by Roli Books
M-75, Greater Kailash-II Market
New Delhi – 110048, India
Ph: +91-11-40682000
E-mail: info@rolibooks.com
Website: www.rolibooks.com

ISBN: 9789349474673

Printed and bound in New Delhi, India